light fighter

A DEVOTIONAL GUIDE FOR SOLDIERS
and all who fight for the light

And this is the judgment, that the light has come into the world, and people loved darkness rather than light because their deeds were evil. For all who do evil hate the light and do not come to the light, so that their deeds may not be exposed. But those who do what is true come to the light, so that it may be clearly seen that their deeds have been done in God.

John 3:19-21

By
Chaplain (COL) James M. Fogle-Miller
Florida Army National Guard, Retired

Dedicated to all those who fight for the Light
With a special thanks to the men and women
of the Army National Guard and the families
who stand behind them, especially my own.

pilgrimage

Factoryville, PA

Light Fighter: A Devotional Guide for Soldiers and All Who Fight for the Light

Published by Pilgrimage Educational Resources
P.O. Box 538, Factoryville, PA 18419
www.simplyapilgrim.com

Printed in the United States of America

Executive Developer: Benjamin J. Wilhite
Edited by Jesse Wilhite
Graphic design by Lance Young (ygraphicdesign.com)

ISBN-13 978-0-61573-341-8
ISBN 0-6157-3341-7

10 9 8 7 6 5 4 3 2 1

First published by the author, April 2000. Incorporates all of a previous devotional guide entitled SOD-G Special Operations Devotional Guide, which was printed in April 1995. Third printing, May, 2004.

This volume is the fourth printing of this work.

Special Sales
Most Pilgrimage Educational Resources books are available at special quantity discounts in bulk by ministry and educational organizations. Works designed for military ministry are, at times, available at deep discounts or for free, as funding is available. For more information or to contribute to funding military ministry distribution, please email info@simplyapilgrim.com or call 570.504.1463.

Our deepest gratitude is owed the men and women of the US Armed Forces past, present and future. This project is only one fruit of your dedication and sacrifice.

Digital copies of this resource and other military edition spiritual resources are available online at:

www.MilitaryDevotional.com

This project was sponsored by:

contents

* These devotions use only the Hebrew Scriptures

THE GUIDE

1. To provide devotions which a soldier may use when he or she must provide spiritual care for herself or himself, or for other soldiers, especially in the absence of a chaplain.

2. To use the Hebrew and Christian scriptures in a humorous way to build spiritual awareness and recognition of the total army team, conventional and unconventional, reserve component (which includes the National Guard!) and active component. (Heartfelt thanks go to the men of 3/20 SFG(A) and the men and women of the 53rd Infantry Brigade, all of the Florida Army National Guard, who inspired a number of the devotions.)

3. To place emergency religious care instructions in leadership hands.

4. To give families a tool that may help them understand more about a soldier's life.

HOW TO USE THE GUIDE:

: Choose a devotion. Start at the beginning and take them in order, or skip around. If it's a short deployment, do one a day. If it's a long haul, there are 52 devotions, enough for a year, if you take them one per week. Read the title word and its definition, then consider the story that accompanies it.

: A section called *For Reflection* is part of each devotion. Think about your personal answers to the questions that are asked in this section. You may want to get with others and share your responses.

: Each devotion has a scripture reference. If you have a Bible, look up and read the entire reference.

: Some or all of the reference is quoted for those without Bibles. Read the biblical material and compare it to the story that preceded it.

: Devotions marked in the Table of Contents with an asterisk use only the Hebrew Scriptures and contain no references to Jesus. Jewish soldiers may find them to be usable devotions.

: Prayer is a good way to begin and end your devotion time.

: Emergency prayers (for the dying and the dead) are found in the appendix. Protestant, Catholic, Jewish, Eastern Orthodox, and Muslim faiths are covered.

: To help the reader remember the big picture, this guide is divided into sections:

1. Army Life
2. Tabs and Badges
3. Command and Staff
4. Support Company
5. Others (Miscellaneous)
6. Army Values

Sections Two through Five were part of the original devotional guide entitled, **SOD-G Special Operations Devotional Guide.**

light fighter

SECTION ONE:::
ARMY LIFE

light fighter

Aa DEFINITION:::

One of God's people, who fights for the light, i.e. on behalf of the good. Alternatively, straight-leg, non-mechanized infantry, known for traveling light, particularly without "snivel gear" (gore-tex parkas, etc.) and whose informal motto is, "Fight light and freeze at night."

SCRIPTURE:::
Luke 9:1-6

Then Jesus called the twelve together and gave them power and authority over all demons to cure diseases, and he sent them out to proclaim the kingdom of God and to heal. He said to them, "Take nothing for your journey, no staff, nor bag, nor bread, nor money – not even an extra tunic. Whatever house you enter, stay there and leave from there. Wherever they do not welcome you, as you are leaving that town shake the dust off your feet as a testimony against them." They departed and went through the villages, bringing the good news and curing diseases everywhere.

STORY:::

They were the first light fighters. Not only did they fight for the light, they traveled far lighter than any modern day light fighter. Their commander sent them out with instructions to take no equipment, to live off the land, and to by-pass trouble spots on their way to rescue people who were held captive. It did not seem like a formula for success, but it worked!

They went into hostile territory. When the indigenous population did not welcome them, they continued to march, searching for people and places to support their operations. Wherever they were welcomed, their words set people free from a host of evils. It was a proud time to be a light fighter, and they thought their commander would be with them forever, leading them one day into the country's capital, where he would be crowned king.

Their commander trained them well. They were good at what they did. Those first light fighters did more than seize their objective. They projected a power so strong it made friends out of enemies and brought peace to the world. They were the first light fighters and Jesus was the commander who sent them out.

FOR REFLECTION:::

When you travel light, what are the first things you leave behind?

What are the things you always take with you, no matter what?

In what ways have you been trained spiritually to meet the challenges ahead?

What (or whose) power do you carry with you?

What spiritual weapons are essential for you to take?

May any of these be left safely behind?

Aa DEFINITION:::

The condition of being safe from undergoing or causing hurt, injury, or loss; a device on a military apparatus that prevents it from being fired accidentally. The responsibility of every commander; an additional duty usually assigned to a junior officer who routinely reminds people who aren't listening to be safe.

SCRIPTURE:::
Psalm 78: 52-53

Then [God] led out his people...and guided them in the wilderness.... [God] led them in safety, so that they were not afraid; but the sea overwhelmed their enemies.

STORY:::

It had been a difficult campaign. The division still staggered under its burden. Nearby, the river had run with blood. Famine stalked the land. Flies and disease were everywhere around them. No one in the division could imagine anything worse. A warning order prepared them to move on short notice. They were to carry only minimal supplies and march on foot through the desert, then execute a water crossing under enemy harassment with no bridge and no boats available. Should they survive that, a hostile, forbidding wilderness still stood between them and home. The warning order for the movement specified that only the bare essentials would be carried. All field trains remained behind.

In the midst of this came one who guided the division to safety. Every time they seemed trapped by pursuing forces, a route opened. When the last limits of hunger and thirst were reached, supplies of food and water appeared. It wasn't the division commander who led, but the one upon whom even the commander depended. In spite of every-thing done by the one who led, that one was quickly forgotten whenever the people reached a place of safety.

Field trains: supplies and the means to deliver supplies.

We often take safety for granted, until an accident happens. Look around at all the things you take for granted. How many blessings do you already have?

Some people find safety boring, but in the Bible it is a sign of God's presence (the word safety appears 49 times in the Bible with all but two of those times found in the Hebrew Bible). Have you ever been saved from death or injury because you paid attention to a boring safety routine like buckling a seat belt, making sure a weapon was clear, double-checking a rappelling rig, etc.?

You are a "military apparatus." What device must you set to prevent yourself from "firing accidentally" (for example, losing your temper inappropriately)?

Think of the times God has been present with you. Give thanks that God leads us in safety and that He is our safety.

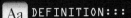

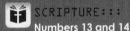

DEFINITION:::

To explore an area to obtain information (as about an enemy); reconnoiter; to find by making a search; member of a reconnaissance force who enters enemy territory to locate enemy units, assess capabilities, pinpoint terrain features, and reports findings back to higher headquarters.

SCRIPTURE:::
Numbers 13 and 14

The Lord said to Moses, "Send men to spy out the land... which I am giving the Israelites; ...every one a leader among them." Moses sent them... and said to them, "Go up into the hill country, and see what the land is like, and whether the people who live in it are strong or weak, whether they are few or many, and whether the land they live in is good or bad, and whether the towns that they live in are unwalled or fortified, and whether the land is rich or poor... Be bold, and bring some of the fruit of the land."

STORY:::

Each one of the twelve was handpicked, already recognized among their units as leaders. They were brought together for a scouting mission. Little more than a squad-sized element, their orders sent them into enemy-held land to find out the numerical strength of the OPFOR, gauge their level of training, check fortifications, determine the amount of cover available, and note indigenous food supplies. It wasn't a quick hit-and-run mission. It was a long patrol, 40 days worth.

Everyone survived the mission. When they arrived at headquarters to be debriefed, everyone gathered around to listen. You could have heard a pin drop as they talked. It sounded good at first. Fresh food to augment MREs, plenty of trees for concealment, good avenues of approach. Hopes began to soar. Maybe the end was in sight!

Then the report changed. Lots of fortifications—in every town! Soldiers were numerous, well trained, and huge! Ten of the scouts ended their report with the comment, "We are not able to go up against them. They are stronger than we are."

Two of the twelve recommended immediate attack. "Let's do it now, we can take these guys!" they said. They had no more data available to them than did the other ten. What made them different was inside them. Where others had fear, they had confidence. It was a matter of faith and it made them bold where the others held back. The attack, as it turned out, was postponed. The ten who got their way got something more. They were relieved of duty and died of disease. The other two lived long lives, one becoming a wealthy land owner and the other rising to four star level, eventually commanding the postponed invasion and leading the way to an era of peace.

Recall times when the other team looked unbeatable. What happened when you played the game?

How hard is it to believe in yourself when your opponent looks bigger and better equipped? What helps you trust your chain of command's assurances that you have the advantage?

When you are the scout, how do you keep up your spirit and find ways to win? Do you look for ways to say, "Yes!" to God, or do you keep finding reasons for saying, "No!"?

Aa DEFINITION:::

A device used by aerial rescue teams to push through the multiple layers of jungle foliage and extract downed pilots or critically wounded soldiers.

SCRIPTURE:::
Luke 19:1-10

When Jesus came to the place, he looked up and said to him, "Zacchaeus, hurry and come down; for I must stay at your house today." So he hurried down and was happy to welcome him. All who saw it began to grumble and said, "Jesus has gone to be the guest of one who is a sinner." Zacchaeus stood there and said to the Lord, "Look, half of my possessions, Lord, I will give to the poor; and if I have defrauded anyone of anything I will pay back four times as much." Then Jesus said to him, "Today salvation[a word which means healing, being made whole, or even rescued] has come to this house, because Zacchaeus too is a son of Abraham. For the Son of Man came to seek out and save the lost.

STORY:::

Everything had been going so well. The mission had been a complete success. Bombs dropped. Target destroyed. Only a few more minutes till "feet wet" and safety. Then radar lock! SAMs fired! Hit, going down! Punch out! Good chute. Thank God it worked! I'm going through the trees! Who will ever find me in this jungle?

Overhead the wingman, after destroying the SAM site, circled and radioed the report that launched the search-and-rescue chopper. Now it was a race to see who would reach the downed pilot first, the angel of mercy chopper or the enemy. What a difference it made to have a friend overhead to pinpoint the location, drive off enemy patrols, call in additional help, and guide in the rescue team.

This time it was easy. The only obstacle turned out to be the jungle itself. There was no place to land the chopper and an ordinary rescue collar would simply bounce off the branches of three layers of jungle forest. Where nothing else gets through, the jungle penetrator makes it. Through all the obstacles it pushes until it reaches the downed pilot. Then up out of the wilderness, away from the clutches of the enemy, another lost soul is rescued.

SAM: surface-to-air missile

Feet wet: For a Naval Aviator, it meant back out over the water, away from land-based dangers.

When have you found yourself "shot down", with everything looking bad?

Think about how it felt to have a friend who stayed with you, even when they couldn't help you directly. What would it have meant to you if someone had reached through all your troubles and helped you out of them?

Have you put up layers that keep out family, friends, and God? God searches us out, especially when we are lost, and the best jungle penetrator of all, Jesus, can get through anything to reach us. All we have to do is grab hold – and that's an act of faith.

DEFINITION:::
To lose water or moisture; become dry.

SCRIPTURE:::
John 4:7,9,10-11,13-15
The woman said to him, "Sir, you have no bucket, and the well is deep. Where do you get that living water?" Jesus said to her, "Everyone who drinks of this water will be thirsty again, but those who drink of the water I will give them will never be thirsty. The water that I will give will become in them a spring of water gushing up to eternal life." The woman said to him, "Sir, give me this water..."

STORY:::
The orientation at the Jungle Operations Training Center at Fort Sherman, Panama, made it clear. One key to jungle survival was to stay hydrated. Carry water, purify water, but most of all drink water. It seemed easy.

But there were stretches where pausing to drink was awkward. The water in some of the streams didn't look like anything you'd want to drink, purified or not. Water sitting in the canteen got hot and hard to swallow. Plus there were times when your stomach seemed full even though sweat drenched your uniform and poured like rain from your face.

There were plenty of excuses for becoming dehydrated. In fact, the only way to stay hydrated, to truly keep healthy, was to drink water even when you didn't feel like it, didn't think you needed to, when you weren't feeling thirsty, and when you plain just didn't want to do it. Then, when the difficult moments came, you didn't become a heat casualty.

How well hydrated are you in your spiritual life? That is, how is your church life, prayer life, fellowship of faith time, etc.? If a tough moment came now, would you cramp up, go clammy with exhaustion, or stroke out?

Do you keep drinking of the living water that Jesus offers, even when you think you do not need to do so? When was the last time you asked Jesus for his living water?

What excuses do you use for not staying hydrated spiritually? Is your Christian life like a spring of water gushing up to eternal life inside you or is it more like a stagnant pond? What will you do to help the water flow again?

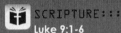

DEFINITION:::

The absence of all magnitude or quantity; a state of total absence or neutrality; the lowest point; the setting or adjustment of the sights of a firearm that causes it to shoot to point of aim at a desired range.

SCRIPTURE:::
Luke 9:1-6
1 Peter 2:9-10

But you are a chosen race, a royal priesthood, a holy nation, God's own people, in order that you may proclaim the mighty acts of him who called you out of darkness into his marvelous light. Once you were not a people; but now you are God's people; once you had not received mercy, but now you have received mercy.

STORY:::

How'd ya do?" they asked each other as they came off the ARF (Automatic Record Fire) range. Excitement and enthusiasm beamed from some eyes. Other soldiers kept their eyes down, as if avoiding looking at others somehow would make themselves invisible. The behavior marked the difference between excellence and the failure to meet even the minimum standard.

Up in the range control tower the computer printed out their scores, but the soldiers knew already whether they had done well or poorly. They waited to find out for certain the category into which they fell. Would they be Expert, Sharpshooter or Marksman? Even worse, did they bolo, fail to qualify?

This particular day, a crisp, cool November day at the ranges, the number of bolo's was high. Savvy NCOs knew the reason before some of the soldiers ever stepped on the qualification range. They talked about it among themselves as they watched:

"Didja see how they were jerking triggers rather than squeezin' like we told 'em to do?"

"Yeah, and the way they were breathing. How many times do we have to tell them about their breathing?"

"That's nothing! I watched a whole batch that never had good spot welds. No way they had good sight pictures!"

"You got that right! They said they were zeroed, but I could see some bad scores coming!"

"These bolos come from poor PMI (Pre-Marksmanship Instruction) and goofin' off on the zero range. That's where we gotta fix this one."

"Yeah, we'll turn this around in a hurry."

AUTHOR'S NOTE:::

Without God, we are not a people. We bolo. With God, we're zeroed. We are called to proclaim God's mighty acts. That's why we are "Light Fighters." Our marksmanship on this stuff often has been pretty poor. But God sent Jesus. That's the mercy we received. Accepting that mercy, that love, and learning how to share it with others, is the PMI and zero range work that makes us Experts on the spiritual record fire range. I pray you're "qualified."

FOR REFLECTION:::

When was the last time you zeroed your spiritual weapons? How much do you pay attention during pre-marksmanship instruction (worship, Bible study, fellowship groups, etc.), and how much do you let your mind wander because you've heard it all before?

The Holy Spirit is sometimes called the breath of God. How do you fill up with and release that breath before you fire? When the pressure is on, it takes discipline to squeeze rather than jerk the trigger. What are you doing to keep that discipline strong?

If you went to a spiritual record fire range would you qualify? How well would you score? Why?

Aa DEFINITION:::

A person sentenced to imprisonment for life; a person who makes a career of one of the armed forces; a person who has made a life-long commitment (as to a way of life).

SCRIPTURE:::
Matthew 5:11, 14-16

"Blessed are you when people revile you and persecute you and utter all kinds of evil against you falsely on my account. You are the light of the world. A city built on a hill cannot be hid. No one after lighting a lamp puts it under the bushel basket, but on the lampstand, and it gives light to all in the house. In the same way, let your light shine before others, so that they may see your good works and give glory to your Father in heaven."

STORY:::

Not that long ago soldiers received a serial number when they joined the Army. Today we use Social Security numbers, but then it was different. You could tell by someone's serial number whether they had been drafted or were career soldiers. A serial number beginning with the letters RA marked one as Regular Army, as a lifer. So did low numbered decals. They had a white background and red numerals for enlisted soldiers, blue numerals for officers. The lower the number the more senior the soldier, and senior meant lifer.

Lifer is a good word, but that day it came out ugly. The boys were walking along the road to the PX. The oncoming convertible, with a low, blue-numbered decal marked the civilian-clothed driver as a senior officer. Sharp salutes came from soldiers who saw the decal and the driver, but something else was thrown by one of the boys.

"Lifer!" he shouted, with a voice full of hate and venom. Brake lights came on, slowing the car and leaving the driver within speaking range. Both boys cringed. This could be trouble. One of them knew the decal's number meant this was the commanding general. "Why'd you do that?" he hissed at his friend, as they waited for what looked like a royal chewing out.

When he turned in his seat you could see a hint of sadness in his eyes, showing the words had hit some spot deep within him. When he spoke, it was with a soft voice, partly wistful, but also firm and filled with conviction. He addressed the boy who had spoken and simply said, "That's right, son, and I'm proud of it."

Neither boy knew it at the time, but they had just learned lessons in leadership: patience; the power of a strong calling; and the ability to stand as a witness to what one believes.

When people make fun of you for being a soldier, or being a Christian, how do you respond?

What things can you do or say that invite people to understand and to change? What helps you neither give in to name calling in return nor give up on the name caller?

How can you represent the best of your beliefs even in the midst of persecution or ridicule? Are you a lifer for God?

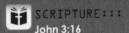

DEFINITION:::

Forming the base or essence, fundamental, constituting or serving as the starting point.

SCRIPTURE:::
John 3:16

"For God so loved the world that he gave his only Son, so that everyone who believes in him may not perish but may have eternal life."

STORY:::

There hadn't been much time to think about it. One day he heard some friends talking about joining up and he decided to try it, too. At first it didn't seem real. Yeah, the papers were signed, but he went home in his own clothes, slept in his own bed. His bratty brother even teased him about being G.I. Joe.

Now he was in basic training, only it seemed more like harassment than training. His hair was gone. If he had wanted to be a skinhead, he could have done that, but his hair had looked good. Everyone said so. Now it was gone.

Gone, too, was everything that was familiar: his clothes, the food he liked, lounging around the house, hanging out with his friends. Even his sleep schedule was different! Awful was more like it. He had never been a morning person. Now, reveille always came too soon. Even words he thought he understood had different meanings. Rifle exercises had looked like a welcome change on the training schedule. After all, how hard could it be to exercise a rifle? Anything was better than more pushups, or so he had thought.

Most of all, he couldn't figure out how in the world the army could call him and the other trainees privates. There wasn't anything private about basic training. Why, sometimes it seemed like the drill sergeants even knew what he was thinking!

One thing was sure, though. He wasn't a civilian anymore. Graduation from basic training was still in the future. But his choice to join and the training received made him different. Now he could see what it meant to be a soldier.

AUTHOR'S NOTE:::

John 3:16 is the basic training course for Christians. Belief in Jesus makes us Christians. After that step, it's on to the Christian equivalents to AIT, PLDC, BNCOC, ANCOC, and SMA (or OBC, OAC, CAS3, CGSC, and War College).

AIT: Advanced Individual Training
PLDC: Platoon Leader's Development Course
BNCOC: Basic Non-Commissioned Officer's Course
ANCOC: Advanced Non-Com Officer's Course

SMA: Sergeants Major Academy
OBC: Officer Basic Course
OAC: Officer Advanced Course
CAS3: Combined Armed Services and Staff School
CGSC: Command and General Staff Course

Have you made your decision to join with Jesus and become a Christian? Who were the people who helped you decide to join the ranks of believers? How are you helping others to join?

What basic training have you been through as a Christian? What additional training do you need to be all that you can be for God?

Being a soldier has made you different from the civilian you used to be. How has being a soldier of Christ, a Christian, made you different from what you were before?

Headcount

Aa DEFINITION:::
Method of keeping track of the number of soldiers on patrol; means of accounting for the number of soldiers eating at a particular mess hall.

SCRIPTURE:::
Matthew 10:28-31
Do not fear those who kill the body but cannot kill the soul; rather fear him who can destroy both body and soul in hell. Are not two sparrows sold for a penny? Yet not one of them will fall to the ground apart from your Father. And even the hairs on your head are counted. So do not be afraid; you are of more value than many sparrows.

STORY:::
The pilot pulled pitch, lifting the chopper off the LZ (Landing Zone). Quickly the team moved into the wood line, spreading out into a normal patrol formation. Now and again a touch of wind cooled the sweat pouring off each soldier, bringing partial relief to the summer heat.

The open pine forest gave way to dense underbrush. A quick hand-signal from the team leader moved people into single file. Keeping the one ahead in sight grew difficult. Soon a different hand signal, one for headcount, passed up and down the line.

From the front and rear the count passed to the team leader. If the count showed a person to be lost, the team would search for the missing one. If an enemy had slipped into the line, the team would implement defensive procedures.

That evening the team, now off patrol, came to the mess hall. As each soldier filed in, they signed the mess sergeant's headcount sheet. "We use it," he said, "to make sure that we get the right amount of food. It helps us make sure that no one goes hungry."

AUTHOR'S NOTE:::
Thanks to the 3/20 SFG(A) team that took a chaplain on a training patrol and taught me a new hand signal – the one for "great big rattlesnake right beside the trail!" Thanks, also, to the 3/20 mess section. You set a good table.

FOR REFLECTION:::

God sends us signals to help us move through life's forests. How well do you know God's signals? If God passed the headcount signal right now, would you be in line to respond?

If you are not in the file, how far would the team have to search to find you?

How do you feel, knowing that God looks for you?

God also wants you to be fed spiritually. When was your last trip to the "mess hall?" Did you sign the "headcount sheet?"

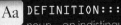

Aa DEFINITION:::
noun – an indistinguishable gathering, jumble.

verb – pucker, wrinkle. An army backpack, to travel by foot while carrying one's ruck or backpack.

SCRIPTURE:::
1 Peter 13-16
Therefore prepare your minds for action; discipline yourselves; set all your hope on the grace that Jesus Christ will bring you when he is revealed. Like obedient children, do not be conformed to the desires that you formerly had in ignorance. Instead, as he who called you is holy, be holy yourselves in all your conduct; for it is written, "You shall be holy, for I am holy."

Biblical Ruck March stories: Exodus, Luke 2:1-7, Luke 9:51
Matthew 2:13-15 and 2:19-23

STORY:::
Ruck March. It looked innocent enough on the training schedule. To the uninformed it meant nothing more than a walk in the woods with a pack on one's back. But careful behind-the-scenes preparations suggested otherwise.

Each ruck had to meet a minimum weight standard. Soldiers considered carefully how to carry every mandatory item without going over the minimum weight.

Feet received attention, too. Boots that merely pinched occasionally in every day wear were going to cause blisters on a sustained march. Some soldiers chose sprays or powders to protect their feet. Others begged moleskin from the medics, or purchased their own at the Post Exchange.

Some talked about their strategy for finishing the ruck march in the required amount of time. "I'm going out fast to get ahead of the power curve on time," declared one. A buddy responded, "No Way! Slow and steady, that's me."

Even the packing of rucks received attention. Put the heavier stuff here and the lighter stuff there. Pack it tight so it doesn't move. Put this where you can get to it quickly. Adjust the straps so it rides just so on your back.

Finally the rucking began. At the starting line everyone looked much the same: well turned out and stepping smartly. Hours and miles later the finish line told a different story. Some beat the time limit easily and still looked fresh. Others made the time, but looked worn out. Still others came in limping, over the time limit, with rucks all askew. Some never finished. Ruck marches do that. They separate the ready, the prepared, from those who are not.

What do you carry with you in the long march through life? What's essential and what can you safely leave out?

How do you exercise (physically, mentally, spiritually, emotionally) to improve your stamina?

Have you packed the emergency stuff where you can quickly get it should you need it?

What's your strategy for your life's ruck? Picture yourself at the finish line. Will you get a passing score? If not, what changes must you make to get it?

SHORT TIMER

Aa DEFINITION:::

One with little time left to serve; a soldier with fewer than 100 days left in the army; one who behaves as if one's time is short.

SCRIPTURE:::
Luke 12:22-26,29-31

He said to his disciples, "Therefore I tell you, do not worry about your life, what you will eat, or about your body, what you will wear. For life is more than food, and the body more than clothing... And do not keep striving for what you are to eat and what you are to drink, and do not keep worrying. For it is the nations of the world that strive after all these things, and your Father knows that you need them. Instead, strive for his kingdom, and these things will be given to you as well."

📖 STORY:::

It was mid-afternoon. Outside the summer sun baked everything. The post bowling alley provided cheap entertainment and welcome air-conditioning. The soldier found entertainment at the bar rather than on the lanes. He'd had lots of "entertainment" before he started going up to complete strangers with his invitation.

"Hey! Shellubrate wif me! I'm short! Jus whenunner uh thowsin days. Onny got 999 moortuhgo. Lemme biyuh uh beer." (Hey! Celebrate with me. I'm short! I just went under a thousand days [left in the army]. I only have 999 more to go. Let me buy you a beer.")

His judgement had gone the way of his language skills, because his offer was to someone well under the drinking age. With a little quick mental arithmetic I translated the number of days to years and began to reply, "999 days! But that's almost three ...."

"Shhuuush! Don' say it. Souns too long tha' way. When frum four digits tuh three. Thas bedder. An don' care how old y'are, I'm buyin' enny way. Godda shellubrate."

The conversation took place over 40 years ago. It was my first conscious encounter with a short timer. Though I declined the beer and went on with my bowling (five games for a dollar and shoes were free), I've never forgotten the conversation.

Years later I would find myself "getting short" in a particularly bad assignment. Only then did I discover that getting short brought a welcome change, one worth celebrating. With my "freedom" in sight I began to live as if I were already free. I didn't go out and get drunk, but I let go of a lot of my worries, and discovered that if I'd done that to begin with, the assignment would not have been so bad. And I remembered a very drunken soldier from a long time ago and that Jesus had talked about living with a short timer's approach.

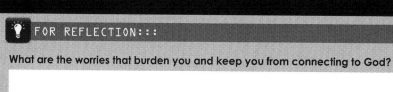

What are the worries that burden you and keep you from connecting to God?

If you were a short timer in your present situation, how would it change your approach?

What keeps you from living more like a short timer (a responsible short timer!)?

light fighter

SECTION TWO:::
TABS AND BADGES

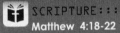
Infantry

Aa DEFINITION:::
That branch of an army consisting of soldiers trained and equipped to fight chiefly on foot. Foot soldiers.

SCRIPTURE:::
Matthew 4:18-22
As he [Jesus] walked by the Sea of Galilee, he saw two brothers, Simon, who is called Peter, and Andrew his brother, casting a net into the sea--for they were fishermen. And he said to them, "Follow me, and I will make you fish for people." Immediately they left their nets and followed him.

STORY:::
There is at least some Biblical evidence that Jesus may have been infantry, or at least infantry-trained. Almost all of his journeys were on foot, for example. Most significant, however, are the words he used in calling his disciples. "Follow me!" he said. Perhaps it was with Jesus that the infantry motto was born.

Note: "Follow Me!" is the Infantry motto.

Remember the times when you have dropped everything you were doing to follow someone else. What was it about the invitation that caught your attention?

What would it take for you to hear Jesus' invitation?

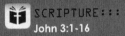
air borne

Aa DEFINITION:::
Carried by or through the air, e.g. bacteria, troops.

SCRIPTURE:::
John 3:1-16
"Now there was a Pharisee named Nicodemus, a leader of the Jews. He came to Jesus by night and said to him, "Rabbi, we know that you are a teacher who has come from God; for no one can do these signs that you do apart from the presence of God." Jesus answered him, "Very truly, I tell you, no one can see the kingdom of God without being born from above.""

STORY:::
Jesus quite likely was more than just straight-leg infantry. There is strong evidence that he was airborne. We know that he came from above. He apparently didn't have much use for "legs" because he told Nicodemus that no one can see the kingdom of God without being born from above. He may even have been a jumpmaster, because Jude refers to him as "the One who can keep you from falling." In the case of Jesus, though, it is not a matter of "Death from Above," but "Life from Above."

Straight-leg, Leg: non-airborne
*Death from Above: U.S. Army Airborne

*For those who wonder:

The Points of Performance
1. Maintain body position and count.
2. Check canopy and gain canopy control.
3. Keep a sharp lookout during descent.
4. Prepare to land.
5. Land.

The Jump Commands
1. Get Ready!
2. Stand Up!
3. Hook Up!
4. Check Static Line!
5. Check Equipment!
6. Sound Off for Equipment Check!
7. Standby!
8. Go!

Every Airborne soldier has made the leap from a plane. Every person has also made the leap into life. Consider your points of performance* during an airborne descent.

Think of ways that they are guidelines for making it through life as well. You might try the same exercise with the jump commands.* (The Society of St. Michael, the patron saint of Airborne soldiers, does this. See your Chaplain if you are interested.).

Ranger

Aa DEFINITION:::
One who ranges; a wanderer; any of a group of soldiers trained for raiding and close combat.

SCRIPTURE:::
Psalm 23
The Lord is my shepherd, I shall not want. He makes me lie down in green pastures; he leads me beside still waters; he restores my soul. He leads me in right paths for his name's sake. Even though I walk through the darkest valley, I fear no evil; for you are with me; your rod and your staff- they comfort me. You prepare a table before me in the presence of my enemies... my cup overflows. Surely goodness and mercy shall follow me all the days of my life and I shall dwell in the house of the Lord my whole life long.

STORY:::
If Jesus is infantry and airborne, as other parts of this devotional guide suggest, might he also be Ranger-qualified? A two-tab man? The direct biblical evidence isn't as conclusive. But a little bit of conjecture builds a strong case.

The Ranger motto is "Lead the Way!" Those exact words are not attributed to Jesus in any of the gospels. However, the church has proclaimed throughout the centuries that there is no place we can go where Jesus has not already gone before us. In life, in death, in life beyond death, Jesus has led the way. His actions made him a ranger.

AUTHOR'S NOTE:::
Soldiers assigned to Airborne units wear a small patch, called a tab, over their unit patch. It spells out the word 'Airborne'. Similarly, graduates of the U. S. Army Ranger School wear a tab that proclaims them to be Ranger-qualified. Thus, Rangers assigned to Airborne units will wear two tabs above their unit patch, one saying 'Airborne', and one saying 'Ranger'.

As a Ranger, Jesus is always leading the way. He is an eternal point man. When have you ignored the signals of your point man and walked into an ambush?

What does it mean to you that Jesus is always out in front?

Special Forces

DEFINITION:::

Special-- of a kind different from others; distinctive, peculiar or unique. Exceptional, extraordinary.

SCRIPTURE:::
Matthew 22:34-40

When the Pharisees heard that he had silenced the Sadducees, they gathered together, and one of them, a lawyer, asked him a question to test him. "Teacher, which commandment in the law is the greatest?" He [Jesus] said to him, "'You shall love the Lord your God with all your heart, and with all your soul, and with all your mind.' This is the greatest and first commandment. And a second is like it: 'You shall love your neighbor as yourself.' On these two commandments hang all the law and the prophets."

STORY:::

Jesus actually was triple-tabbed. Other devotions in this guide talk about his airborne and ranger tabs. Now there is, admittedly, no direct biblical quote to substantiate Jesus being SF. However, in the early days of Special Forces, people were occasionally awarded the Green Beret on the basis of their actual experiences. Consider those of Jesus.

He came and lived among the people. His mission was to win their hearts, minds, and souls. We have his own words about how important it was to love people as we would ourselves like to be loved. He trained the indigenous population to carry his message throughout the countryside. He liberated the oppressed (remember *de opresso liber**) and established methods of unconventional warfare that are still in the manuals today.

The evidence is quite overwhelming. Jesus had to have been Special Forces qualified.

*de opresso liber is the Special Forces motto. It means Liberate the Oppressed.

SF: Special Forces

Triple-tabbed: See the note about tabs in the Ranger devotion. Special Forces qualified soldiers earn a tab that says Special Forces. A Special Forces soldier who is also Ranger-qualified will, when assigned to an Airborne unit, thus wear three tabs. Starting at the top is Special Forces, then Ranger, and last Airborne.

What is the best way to win the hearts of people?

Has God won your heart? If not, what more would you have God do?

Aa DEFINITION:::
Any foundation, base, support, etc.

SCRIPTURE:::
Romans 12:1-8

For by the grace given to me I say to everyone among you not to think of yourself more highly than you ought to think, but to think with sober judgment, each according to the measure of faith which God has assigned. For as in one body we have many members, and not all the members have the same function, so we, who are many, are one body in Christ, and individually we are members one of another. We have gifts that are different according to the grace given to us.

STORY:::
So Jesus may have been triple-tabbed. Is that what made him great? There are plenty of triple-tabbed people who think they are god. Do the tabs and their self-importance make them great?

Seneca, a Roman philosopher and statesman, suggested we look elsewhere to measure the greatness of a person. "None of those who have been raised to a loftier height by riches and honors is really great," he writes. "Why then does he seem great to you? It is because you are measuring the pedestal along with the man."

True greatness is within us. Prizes, awards, fame, honor, rank, qualification badges, or the number of tabs do not create it.

See the notes at the Ranger and Special Forces devotions for an understanding about tabs.

As you measure yourself, are you more pedestal or more person?

What about as others measure you?

How do you think God measures you?

JUMPMASTER

Aa DEFINITION:::

Performs personnel inspections to insure that parachutists are properly rigged for a safe exit from the aircraft. Responsible for the safety of the jumpers, spotting the drop zone, and getting the jumpers on target.

SCRIPTURE:::
Jude 24-25

Now to him who is able to keep you from falling, and to make you stand without blemish in the presence of his glory with rejoicing, to the only God our Savior, through Jesus Christ our Lord, be glory, majesty, power, and authority, before all time and now and forever. Amen.

STORY:::

Everyone has these stories. They're told wherever jumpers gather. Passed on from one generation to the next, they are one way that people learn from the mistakes of others. They are the stories of the time the jumpmaster caught a mistake that would have caused disaster, dismemberment, or discomfort.

- The parachute harness straps were not rigged evenly. One was set on 4, the other on 3. Just an off-kilter chute.
- A tiny bit of nylon showed on the reserve chute. Did changing it prevent a deployment of the chute in the aircraft?
- A misrouted static line would have tied things together and resulted in a towed jumper.
- A tired jumper moved toward the door with the static line around rather than over his arm.

What many people don't know is that Jesus is the greatest jumpmaster of all. He can truly keep us from falling.

FOR REFLECTION:::

What are your stories? Are there some jumpmasters you prefer to check your equipment? What makes them good?

Think about how much confidence a good jumpmaster gives you. What would it be like to have someone who could do a really good jumpmaster personnel inspection on you before you made any leap in life (like changing jobs, getting married, going to school, etc.)?

Scuba

DEFINITION:::

Self-Contained Underwater Breathing Apparatus; refers to the qualification badge worn by those who have completed the rigorous training required.

SCRIPTURE:::

Consider these passages:

1) Zechariah 10:11– They shall pass through the sea of distress, and the waves of the sea shall be smitten.

2) Matthew 4:18ff -- A windstorm arose on the sea. Then he (Jesus) got up and rebuked the wind and the sea, and there was a dead calm.

3) Matthew 14:30-32 -- Beginning to sink, he cried out, "Lord save me!" Jesus immediately reached out his hand and caught him, saying to him, "You of little faith, why did you doubt?"

STORY:::

Difficult as it may be to believe, there is some evidence that scuba courses existed in biblical times. The importance of being able to handle oneself in the water is seen in a number of Bible stories. Between the Hebrew and Christian scriptures there are over 1,400 references to either the sea, water, waters, river, rivers, or lake.

Look at Genesis 7:18 and following. Four times it says, "the waters prevailed." Scuba-qualified people can tell you how many times in their training they felt that was going to happen to them.

Check out Exodus 14:27 (you may even want to read the whole Exodus story). There it says, "the Lord tossed the Egyptians into the sea."

For you scuba course graduates, how about Revelation 19:20 and 8:9? "These two were thrown alive into the lake of fire." "A third of the sea became blood." Remember those days in your training?

Both the Hebrew and Christian scriptures (i.e. the Old and New Testaments) suggest how to survive times of trial. Each speaks of believing in God with one's whole heart, mind, soul, and strength. Which of those parts of yourself do not yet wholly believe in God?

Each of us, in matters of faith, is already SCUBA-qualified. Each of us has a Self-Contained Universal Believing Apparatus. It's called a heart. And your heart will get you through anything. But you have to believe. What most helps you believe?

PATHFINDER

DEFINITION:::
One who makes known a path or way where none had existed, as in an unknown region, wilderness, etc.

SCRIPTURE:::
Exodus 13:21-22
The Lord went in front of them in a pillar of cloud by day, to lead them along the way, and in a pillar of fire by night, to give them light, so that they might travel by day and by night. Neither the pillar of cloud by day nor the pillar of fire by night left its place in front of the people.

STORY:::
It is appropriate that the Pathfinder qualification badge includes a torch. After all it was by a huge torch (actually a pillar of fire), that God led the people of Israel through the wilderness. It happened this way.

The entire Special Forces community had been involved in an HCA mission there in Egypt. All went well for a long time, but then things turned sour. A change in government found them all held captive, except for Moses, a Pathfinder who had activated his own personal E & R plan.

God sent Moses back on the biggest prisoner rescue mission ever. The exfil plan included one of the most incredible water exits of all time (see the story of the Red Sea). Then it was survival-skill time, with water from rocks, food from heaven, and the Big Pathfinder leading the way with a pillar of fire by night and a pillar of cloud by day. Finally, they made it all the way to the land they dreamed of: the promised land. And the Big Pathfinder made it possible.

HCA: Humanitarian Civic Action

E & R: Escape and Resistance

Exfil: exfiltration (i.e. getting out, the opposite of infiltration)

GSPS: Global Satellite Positioning System (this hand-held unit precisely pinpoints one's location on the earth).

Think of a time when you have felt trapped by circumstances beyond your control. What was it like to begin your escape and find yourself caught between a pursuing army and a deep ocean?

Remember what it is like to be all but lost on land navigation when you suddenly find a key terrain feature. In the pillar of cloud and fire the escaping Israelites had a GP (global positioning) system. Where would God's GPS say you are in your spiritual journey?

Aa DEFINITION:::

A circle of light appearing to surround the sun, the moon, or a comet and resulting from refraction or reflection of light by ice particles in the atmosphere; the aura of glory, veneration, or sentiment surrounding an idealized person or thing; qualified for high altitude, low opening parachuting.

SCRIPTURE:::
John 1:2

He (Jesus) was in the beginning with God.

Also:
Luke 2:7 And she gave birth to her firstborn son and wrapped him in bands of cloth, and laid him in a manger, because there was no place for them in the inn.

STORY:::

People in my church were proud of me for completing Jump School. When it was announced that I had earned my wings, the congregation spontaneously broke into applause. Their support gave me a good feeling. But the feeling was short-lived.

After the service one person said, while shaking my hand on the way out of the church, "You've got wings. Too bad you can't get a halo to go with them." I wasn't quick enough to respond, "But I could!"

Jesus, being born from above, is Airborne qualified. What few people stop to realize is that he is also HALO qualified. In fact, he holds the record for the highest altitude (all the way from God), lowest opening (ground level, with Mary, in a stable) jump. If you are HALO qualified, know that Jesus has been there, done that.

And the jumpers leaped, falling comet-like toward the earth, through an occasional cloud filled with icy particles. A circle of light, a halo, surrounded these military free-fall parachutists. And when they landed, they were surrounded by an aura of glory. It was veneration coming from static-line jumpers who dreamed of falling free.

HALO: High Altitude, Low Opening

Have you ever basked so long in the admiration of others that you have gotten a distorted image of yourself?

What brought you back down to earth? How do you keep a halo on straight?

light fighter

SECTION THREE:::
COMMAND
AND STAFF

commander

Aa DEFINITION:::
A person who commands; leader. (Command is defined as "give an order or orders to; direct with authority.")

SCRIPTURE:::
Matthew 8:5-13
Portions are quoted in the STORY section.

STORY:::
Imagine this: Your commander is like Jesus. Sound far-fetched? Then reverse it. Jesus is like a commander.

A Roman centurion (who had charge of 100 soldiers) comes to Jesus asking that his servant be healed. When Jesus said he would come and cure the servant, the centurion told Jesus, "No." He knew Jesus did not need to make the trip because Jesus had the power, the authority, to accomplish his mission from where he was.

So it was that the centurion said to Jesus, "Only speak the word, and my servant will be healed. For I also am a man under authority, with soldiers under me; and I say to one, 'Go,' and he goes, and to another 'Come,' and he comes." And Jesus told his followers that nowhere in Israel had he found such faith. To the centurion he said, "Go; let it be done according to your faith." And the servant was healed in that hour.

Are your orders only for others? Can you command yourself?

What prayers and spiritual practices will help you bear the stress and loneliness of command?

What are you doing as a commander to see that your subordinates are healed?

What are you doing that they will fully understand only after you have been reassigned (as was the case with Jesus and his disciples)?

Command Sergeant Major

DEFINITION:::

The dictionary defines sergeant major as the highest-ranking noncommissioned officer. It does not define Command Sergeant Major, perhaps because the position defies definition.

SCRIPTURE:::
2 Peter 1:19

1) 2 Peter 1:19 So we have the prophetic message more fully confirmed. You will do well to be attentive to this as to a lamp shining in a dark place, until the day dawns and the morning star rises in your hearts.

2) John 19:1-2 Then Pilate took Jesus and had him flogged. And the soldiers wove a crown of thorns and put it on his head.

STORY:::

At a gathering in the highest halls of power. The commanding general (CG), who wore all the stars in the universe, announced that Operation Down to Earth required a general officer to become enlisted. Only when this gulf was crossed by someone who truly understood the commanding general's love for the troops, and who was truly one of the troops, could the message be made clear.

The CG's own son was chosen. Of flag rank himself, equal in fact to the CG, he was sometimes referred to by his rank insignia: The Morning Star -- the brightest, highest star of all.

Down to Earth he came as a regular Joe Snuffy: washing people's feet; doing carpentry work; leading a squad-sized element; recruiting and teaching others; and practicing field medicine. But his message of the CG's love was not understood, so they took him out and flogged him. The stripes he earned progressing through all the MOS skill levels were now carved into his flesh.

Then they made him wear a wreath. No one believed he was really the CG's son, entitled to wear a star in his own right. And so the wreath, really a crown of thorns, was placed upon him, exacting another price in blood.

Then he was killed. When it was over people slowly began to understand. Here was someone who spoke for and to everybody, even God, and the stripes, wreath, and star were symbols of the man. His name was Jesus.

MOS: Military Occupational Specialty

CSM: Command Sergeant Major. The rank insignia for a CSM has three stripes up and three stripes (rockers) down. In the center is a star, surrounded by a wreath.

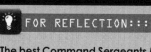

The best Command Sergeants Major help messages from on high to be understood. They also intercede on behalf of the troops, collectively and individually. What does your spiritual CSM (Jesus) need to make clear to you about God's love?

What are you worried about that you need him to tell God? Jesus is an approachable CSM with an open-door policy. Go in now and tell him everything you need. By the way, we call that prayer -- and it works.

DEFINITION:::
Concerned with carrying out duties, functions, etc. or managing affairs; an officer who is chief assistant to the commanding officer (Yes, that's what the dictionary says).

SCRIPTURE:::
Luke 22:39-42
He (Jesus) came out and went, as was his custom, to the Mount of Olives; and the disciples followed him. When he reached the place, he said to them, "Pray that you may not come into the time of trial." Then he withdrew from them about a stone's throw, knelt down, and prayed, "Father, if you are willing, remove this cup from me; yet, not my will but yours be done."

STORY:::
Who in their right mind would want to be an XO? There you are, responsible for making things happen but always subject to someone else telling you how you have to do it. Then there are all those people who want to know, "On whose authority are you doing these things?" Translated, that means, "Is this your hare-brained scheme or does the Commander really want us to do that?"

Well, Jesus has been there, too. People were constantly challenging his authority. Some did not believe his power came from God (Jesus' commander). Others thought Jesus to be the chief demon. (Now that fits with what lots of people think about an XO.)

But the essence comes when Jesus is in prayer during his last days. He knows the OP Plan. It is all painfully clear. So he goes to the Commander and says, "If there is any way we can do this differently, let it be so." When he hears that the plan, as written, becomes the OP Order the next day, Jesus responds, "Airborne, Sir!" And he goes out and gives his life to ensure the success of the operation.

OP: Operations

XO: Executive Officer

Describe a time when you carried out an order with which you disagreed. Did it turn out differently than you expected?

What do you have to do to let someone else really be in charge? What must you do to let God be in control of your life?

 STAFF

DEFINITION:::
A group of officers serving a military commanding officer in an advisory and administrative capacity without combat duties or command.

SCRIPTURE:::
Proverbs 11:14
Proverbs 11:14 -- Where there is no guidance, an army falls, but in an abundance of counselors there is safety.

Proverbs 15:22 -- Without counsel, plans go wrong, but with many advisers they succeed.

Proverbs 20:18 -- Plans are established by taking advice; wage war by following wise guidance.

STORY:::
They come kicking and screaming. Special Forces soldiers hate leaving their team and going to battalion. Infantry types hate leaving command positions and moving to staff responsibilities. The universal cry is, "Please! Don't send me there! I'm not a staff weenie."

No one wants to do it, but someone has to manage personnel assets. No one wants to do it, but someone has to put all of the intel puzzle pieces together. No one wants to do it, but someone has to coordinate plans, operations, and training. No one wants to do it, but somebody has to get beans and bullets in the right places for the right number of people. No one wants to do the very jobs that are essential if anyone is to complete the mission.

The staff is to the commander, is to the teams, and is to subordinate units, what the jumpmaster is to jumpers.

FOR REFLECTION:::

Remember the times when someone with a slightly different point of view helped you find a solution you had not considered. Has there ever been a time when you would have forgotten something, but for someone else's reminder? Whose example guides you in what you do?

Aa DEFINITION:::

Handles personnel matters; is concerned that every soldier in the unit be accounted for in the daily strength report.

SCRIPTURE:::
Luke 15:3-7

What man of you, having a hundred sheep, if he has lost one of them, does not leave the 99 in the wilderness, and go after the one which is lost, until he finds it? And when he has found it, he lays it on his shoulders, rejoicing. And when he comes home, he calls together his friends and his neigh-bors, saying to them, 'Rejoice with me, for I have found my sheep which was lost. Just so... there will be more rejoicing in heaven over one sinner who repents than over 99 righteous persons who need no repentance.

STORY:::

In the parable of the lost sheep Jesus made clear his abilities as the best S-1 ever. The way the story is told there is a unit formation for accountability purposes. In the process of taking the count it is discovered that one individual is missing. While there are 99 who still need to be fed, sheltered, and given direction, the concern of the good S-1 is to find the one who is lost.

The frantic effort to search for the missing so that the final count is both correct and complete mirrors what happens in the S-1 section when the strength reports don't add up. The S-1 flies into a frenzy trying to find the soldier who is lost. Whether the loss be real or simply an administrative error, no effort is spared until the numbers once again tally correctly.

There is no place we can go where the big S-1 in the Sky forgets us or drops us from the count.

Think of death, the "final retirement." Will you receive an honorable discharge?

If you are headed toward a less-than-honorable discharge, what would turn you around? (Repentance doesn't mean feeling sorry. It means turning toward God.)

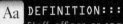

DEFINITION:::
Staff officer or section responsible for military intelligence; Receives, processes, and analyzes all intelligence sources to complete an intelligence preparation of the battlefield.

SCRIPTURE:::
John 4:7-30
Jesus answered her, "If you knew the gift of God, and who it is that is saying to you, 'Give me a drink,' you would have asked him, and he would have given you living water.' ...Jesus said to her, "You are right in saying, 'I have no husband': for you have had five husbands, and the one you have now is not your husband." ...Then the woman left her water jar and went back to the city. She said to the people, "Come and see a man who told me everything I have ever done! He cannot be the Messiah, can he?"

STORY:::
HUMINT (Human intelligence) was one of Jesus' big things. He could look right at people and, with no interrogation at all, know everything about them. Time and again he demonstrated this valuable capability.

On any number of occasions he recognized that enemy agents actually controlled some of the people he encountered. With simple words of command he counteracted their brainwashing and restored them to his own force. The scriptures called this "casting out demons."

Particularly impressive was his complete analysis of the woman at the well. Jesus knew how many times she had been married, with whom she was currently sleeping, and everything else she had done. This was without ever asking her a single question. As the Supreme Intelligence Analyst, he also gave the woman the means to join the good side and draw living water from a well that would never run dry.

What things inside you would Jesus name as your secret shames or fears? Think how the naming of them brings them to light.

What word would Jesus have to speak to heal and forgive you? Hear him speak that word.

STORY:::

Without a doubt Jesus was the best S-3 ever to walk the earth. His careful training and outstanding operations plan ensured that the gospel would spread around the world.

He took 12 carefully chosen disciples, gave them numerous periods of intense instruction, personally demonstrated how they were to accomplish their preaching and healing missions, and with a short, concise verbal operations order sent them on their way to do the same thing with others. What started as a small group of twelve followers grew over the years to include billions of people. And in the nearly 2,000 years since that first op order was implemented no one has come up with a better one. S-3 personnel need look no further than the Master to find an example to follow.

God has given each of us a mission tasking (MITASK). Have you worked up courses of action, done a brief back, prepared your equipment, rehearsed the mission and launched? Or are you instead locked into a training cycle, unready to be certified, validated, or deployed as part of the team?

What will make you ready? What are your specified and implied tasks? What do you need to carry out your MITASK?

Aa DEFINITION:::

Logistician; supplies beans and bullets; keeps the troops fed.

SCRIPTURE:::
Matthew 14:13-22

Jesus said to them, "...you give them something to eat." They replied, "We have nothing here but five loaves and two fish." And he said, "Bring them here to me." Then he ordered the crowds to sit down on the grass. Taking the five loaves and two fish, he looked up to heaven, and blessed and broke the loaves, and gave them to the disciples, and the disciples gave them to the crowds. And all ate and were filled.

STORY:::

The welfare of the troops is the primary concern for any S-4. Do they have everything they need to complete their mission? Particularly, can they be fed wherever they are and whatever they are doing? For today's S-4 Jesus stands as a shining example. There are at least two supply stories recorded in the Christian scriptures.

First, there was a big family support activity. Everyone was there having a great time. Suddenly they noticed that the kegs had run dry. Jesus saved the day. He took several large containers of water (some 60 gallons worth) and changed it all into wine so that the family day could continue. But the really great S-4 miracle was the feeding of the multitude.

The people had been going for some time in an up-tempo operational mode. The day was drawing to a close. They were all hungry, over 5,000 of them. All they had on hand were five packages of shelf stable bread and two MRE's. Jesus took that small amount and without going to a warehouse, without any organic transportation assets and no lead planning time, used it to feed every swinging Joe who was there.

If you are an S-4 type, you have no better example than Jesus.

Have you ever been in a place you had very little but shared it anyway? How do you feel when you share? Remember a time when you thought there was nothing and all at once there was more than you needed. God's grace is enough to feed us all.

Aa
DEFINITION:::

The staff officer or section responsible for those functions that fall under the heading of civil affairs. Among the 20 different functional specialties are: dislocated civilians; public health; public safety; and public welfare.

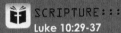

SCRIPTURE:::
Luke 10:29-37

But wanting to justify himself, he asked Jesus, "And who is my neighbor?

"...Which of these three, do you think, was a neighbor to the man who fell into the hands of the robbers?" He said, "The one who showed him mercy." Jesus said to him, "Go and do likewise."

STORY:::

It has happened more than once. In fact it's an old, old story. Not long ago it was among the Kurdish people in Iraq. It happened again in Somalia. Haiti has experienced it, too.

Regular people, going about their own business, harming no one, are robbed, beaten, and left to die, either of their wounds or starvation. They are at the mercy of armed thugs. Otherwise decent law-abiding citizens are unwilling to lift a hand to help them.

Then along comes an outsider, someone actually despised by the people of the country. With great care and concern the victim's needs are met. Medical care is arranged. Food and lodging are found. Follow-on support is promised and delivered.

This process defines the concept of good neighbor. And the world, by just such efforts, is made a better place to live.

Do you believe compassion is a natural human response to someone who is suffering? (The Latin root words for compassion mean "to suffer with.")

How much courage does it take to stop and help today? Remember, blood from the wounds may carry disease. The accident even may be faked, set up as a terrorist trap. What will you do?

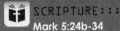

Aa DEFINITION:::

Provides routine and emergency medical care; prevents diseases, treats wounds; dispenses pills; keeps people going.

SCRIPTURE:::
Mark 5:24b-34

And immediately the hemorrhage ceased; and she felt in her body that she was healed of her disease. And Jesus, perceiving in himself that power had gone forth from him, immediately turned about in the crowd, and said, "Who touched my garments?" ....the woman... came in fear....and told him the whole truth. And he said to her, "Daughter, your faith has made you well; go in peace, and be healed of your disease."

STORY:::

It is easier to see Jesus as a medic than almost anything else. Throughout the four gospels, stories abound of Jesus healing people. Some 25 times the word "heal" or "healed" is used. "Cured" appears 33 times. That's 58 times altogether.

At the end of John's gospel we are told that all of the miraculous things written about Jesus are just the tip of the iceberg. He puts it this way, "But there are also many other things which Jesus did; were every one of them to be written, I suppose that the world itself could not contain all the books that would be written."

A child lives because an SF medical team was on the spot in the aftermath of Hurricane Andrew. Deployed medics teach basic sanitation techniques and dramatically lower the risk of disease. A soldier lives because a combat lifesaver did the right thing. Chronic pain ends because of diagnosis, referral, and treatment. In all these ways lives are transformed. Pain and suffering are ended. What lies ahead is truly nothing less than new life.

SF: Special Forces

From where does the power to heal come?

If you are a medic, how much healing can you do before you are exhausted? What energy does it take for someone to treat you?

If Jesus were to touch the part(s) of you that needed healing (or the sins that needed to be forgiven) what would he touch? Close your eyes and feel that touch.

light FightEr

SECTION FOUR:::
SUPPORT
COMPANY

: RIGGER
: COMMO
: MESS
: MAINTENANCE

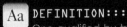

Rigger

Aa DEFINITION:::
One qualified by train-
ing to pack military para-
chutes; one who wears the
qualification badge that displays a parachute, the word
rigger, and wings

SCRIPTURE:::
Psalm 91:11-12

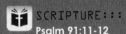

For he will give his angels
charge of you to guard you
in all your ways. On their
hands they will bear you
up, lest you dash your foot
against a stone.

STORY:::
He didn't look like an angel, but then
sometimes it's hard to tell. Standing in the back
of the deuce-and-a-half he smiled and joked
as the jumpers came to pick up their chutes.
"No, don't take that one," he exclaimed to the
overbearing officer, "Yours is that one, with the
'X' on it."

I stood to one side and watched. Still a "leg",
this was my first encounter with riggers, that
strange breed of people with an extra set of
wings.

The harness shed was different. Black hats
yelled. Things moved quickly. One JMPI
followed another. Occasionally the cry went
up, the jumpmaster yelling at the top of his
voice, "Rigger!" Then over trotted someone
who seemed calm in the midst of the storm.
Carefully, deliberately the rigger poked,
prodded, and decided if the chute needed to
go for re-packing.

Then came the opportunity to watch the
riggers at work. Long tables filled the room.
Up and down each one went riggers. Strong,
sure hands followed a prescribed sequence
to make sure each parachute was properly
packed. Quiet pride was evident on each
face as one of the riggers looked up and said,
"Chaplain, we'll never let you fall." That's when
it hit me: angels.

JMPI: Jumpmaster Personnel Inspection. Each
jumper receives a JMPI from two different
jumpmasters before jumping.

Leg: not airborne qualified.

FOR REFLECTION:::

Think of all the times when you entrust your life to someone else's work. If you trust your life to a rigger you've never met, why not trust your soul to God, whom you have seen in Jesus? Think about times when you have made leaps of faith and God has kept you from falling. Have there been times when it seemed your main effort did not work but you found what you had in reserve got you through? When did you last thank the Big Rigger?

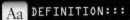

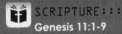 DEFINITION:::

1. an act or instance of transmitting; 2. information communicated; 3. a process by which information is exchanged between individuals through a common system of symbols. 4. (plural) a system (as of telephones) for communicating.

SCRIPTURE:::
Genesis 11:1-9

They said, "Come, let us build ourselves a city, and a tower with its top in the heavens, and let us make a name for ourselves... The Lord came down to see the city and the tower, which mortals had built. And the Lord said, "Look, they are one people, and they have all one language; and this is only the beginning of what they will do; nothing they propose will now be impossible for them. Come, let us go down and confuse their language there, so that they will not understand one another's speech."

STORY:::

Once there was a time when everyone could make Commo. There was no concern about compatible equipment, having correct freqs, or needing a CEOI for passwords and other instructions. Whenever anyone spoke, they were understood.

Because they always made commo, they began to say to themselves, "Let's build a commo tower that reaches to the heavens. Then we will be like God." That's when God took notice.

God said, "If they perfect this next generation of communications technology it will be only the beginning of what they can do. They'll be able to do anything they want and they will truly think they are gods." So God created a nightmare of commo difficulties: weird take-off angles on tropo shots; satellites that lose orbit; jamming techniques; incompatible equipment; and a host of different languages and accents.

And today's commo section? Well, the 18 Echoes and 31 Charlies take us closer back to that time when all humankind could communicate. In that they are, perhaps, more like God than anyone else.

CEOI: Communication, Electronics Operating Instructions

Freqs: frequencies

18 Echoes and 31 Charlies: communication specialists

Tropo: troposphere

When did you last have a commo check with God?

Commo checks are two-way: did you check to see if you were receiving, or were you just sending?

Answer the same two questions about your earthly loved ones. Which part of your communications network needs maintenance or repair?

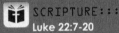

Aa DEFINITION:::

A portion or quantity of food for a meal or a dish; a group of people who regularly have their meals together, as in the army, the meal eaten by such a group, the place where it is eaten.

SCRIPTURE:::
Luke 22:7-20

1) The Last Supper -- Luke 22:7-20
2) Luke 24:13-43 When he [Jesus] was at table with them, he took the bread and blessed, and broke it, and gave it to them. And their eyes were opened and they recognized him; and he vanished out of their sight. They said to each other, "Did not our hearts burn within us while he talked to us on the road, while he opened to us the scriptures?"

STORY:::

You might think it one of the biggest stretches of all to see Jesus in the soldiers of the Mess Section. Actually, it is one of the shortest.

His last evening with his disciples was spent at the local mess. It was upstairs, off the beaten path. The food wasn't much to brag about. There was some bread and a little bit of wine. There Jesus took an ordinary meal and made it an extraordinary event, one that would forever remind us of him, of his body broken for us on the cross, and his blood spilled out for the forgiveness of our sins.

Later, after his resurrection, Jesus met several of his disciples as they were rucking to Emmaus. He fell in with them, but they did not recognize him, even though his conversation stirred their hearts. It was when they sat down at the local mess, shared a table, and broke bread together that they recognized who he was.

Later those same disciples made their rendezvous point with the rest of the team back in Jerusalem. And Jesus stood among them. He ate a piece of fish, showing he was physically resurrected from the dead.

Time and again it was through the Mess that Jesus made himself known to his disciples. It is one place where he still makes himself known to us today.

FOR REFLECTION:::

Think of special meals you have had when it seemed as if there was an unseen presence with you, in addition to those you could see: a holiday meal, a quiet dinner with your loved one; a memorable communion service at church. Recall times in the mess hall when the conversation was so good, you hated to get up and leave. Imagine receiving a piece of bread from the hands of Jesus, who says, "This is for you, my friend." Name the spiritually empty places that bread will fill and bring to life.

maintenance

Aa DEFINITION:::
The act of maintaining, the upkeep of property or equipment.

SCRIPTURE:::
Matthew 25:1-30
...When the foolish took their lamps, they took no oil with them; but the wise took flasks of oil with their lamps... For it is as if a man, going on a journey, summoned his slaves and entrusted his property to them; [the man goes, returns, praises the servants who have done well, then hears from the one who did poorly]. 'Master, I knew you were a harsh man....so I was afraid, and I went and hid your talent in the ground. Here you have what is yours. But his master replied, 'You wicked and lazy slave!....'"

STORY:::
Jesus may have been many things but, apparently, a maintenance section soldier was not one of them. However, over and over again Jesus said that the kingdom of heaven is like a unit with a maintenance section that is humming.

In one story he told about people who were running light sets off of 30kw generators. Half of them were pulling PMCS and keeping adequate fuel supplies on hand. The other half let things slide. They even fell asleep without checking to make sure they'd have the lights when they needed them. Then, in the middle of the night there was an urgent call for the lights. Those who were not ready were left forever in the dark.

Jesus also told about a commander going on TDY who hand-receipted his equipment to three different sections. Two of the sections took great care of it. Because of their maintenance efforts they were able to make even more out of what they had been given. The third section was afraid to use properly what was entrusted to them. They actually ran the equipment into the ground. When the commander returned, he praised the first two sections and gave them even more equipment, training dollars, and other resources. He also took everything from the third section and gave them all Article 15's, making their poor performance part of their permanent records.

PMCS: Preventive Maintenance, Checks and Services

TDY: Temporary Duty

Article 15: Non-Judicial Punishment

 FOR REFLECTION:::

When was the last time you pulled PMCS on your spiritual life?

Do a quick check now: Are you ready for any demand that may be placed upon you? What parts are worn, broken, or missing? What needs tuning or tightening up? Do you need oil or fuel to keep things running smoothly? Is it time for a major overhaul? Where will you go for the work you need done?

light fighter

SECTION FIVE:::
OTHERS

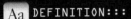

Aa DEFINITION:::

Existing, actual, true, objectively so; not merely seeming, pretended, imagined, fictitious.

SCRIPTURE:::

1 Corinthians 13:12-13

For now we see in a mirror, dimly, but then we shall see face to face. Now I know only in part; then I will know fully, even as I have been fully known. And now faith, hope, and love abide, these three; and the greatest of these is love.

STORY:::

Known simply as "The Wall," the memorial to soldiers killed in the Vietnam War is powerful. The black stone wall, carved into a hillside and engraved with the names of the dead, separates us from them. It also draws us to them.

The print is powerful and poignant. A middle-aged man, briefcase and suit coat on the ground at his side, stands before the wall. One arm is raised, with its outstretched hand poking from the rolled-up sleeves of a white shirt. The hand rests against the wall. The man's head is bowed. Grey hair streaks his beard. Tears dripping from squeezed-shut eyes reflect his pain.

Ghostly images show in the wall. They are soldiers and young. Theirs are the names touched by the outstretched hand. They are untouched by the passing of time. Their wounds are healed. They are whole again, but they feel the man's pain. They huddle around him, concern on their faces, and one raises his hand to touch the one that rests against the wall.

Many times our memories pull us to the wall that separates us from deceased loved ones. We yearn for their touch and reach out to them, choking back tears and feeling once again the pain of their loss. And the promise of our faith is that these loved ones ARE just on the other side, reaching back to us with concern and love. They are with God, where there is no more pain, no more suffering, and no more tears.

Days when we remember are also days to

FOR REFLECTION:::

Think of a deceased loved one whose hand you would like to touch again. Letting all the good memories flood back, feel again the touch of that person and know that they love you. Tell them everything you want them to know. It will be a prayer that they and God hear.

Aa DEFINITION:::
The soldier at the bottom end of the military hierarchy; outranked by everybody; gets all the dirty details.

SCRIPTURE:::
Luke 22:24-27
A dispute also arose among them as to which one of them was to be regarded as the greatest. But he said to them, "..the greatest among you must become like the youngest, and the leader like one who serves. For who is greater, the one who is at the table or the one who serves? Is it not the one at the table? But I am among you as one who serves." Then he poured water into a basin and began to wash the disciples' feet and to wipe them with the towel that was tied around him. (Also **John 13:3-8**)

STORY:::
This "word for the day" clearly belongs near the end of the devotional guide. After all, who is really going to believe that lowly Joe Snuffy is like Jesus? And to be told that Joe Snuffy may be more like Jesus than anyone else? Well, that's hard to swallow. But it's true.

The president-elect had been career military. Along the way he developed a following of twelve really good friends, each a high ranking officer. They were all walking along, headed away from the Pentagon toward Capitol Hill, when two of the generals broke away from the others and came up to the president-elect.

Now, all of the twelve had been arguing about who among them was the greatest, but these two wanted a special favor. One wanted to be the Secretary of the Army and the other wanted to be the Chairman of the Joint Chiefs of Staff. It made the other friends angry when they heard about it. But it made the president-elect sad. So he took a brush, some polish, a little water, and a rag and taught them all another lesson.

He knelt down in front of each one of them and spit-shined their jump boots. When one of them protested, the president-elect said, "If you don't let me do this, you can submit your retirement papers. You won't get to work with me come the big change." And he told them all that to be the greatest meant that they had to be like the lowest Joe Snuffy and willingly serve others.

Which motivates you more: personal ambition or serving others?

Can someone who puts others first truly become great? Can such a person advance in the military?

What must you do to keep Joe Snuffy alive in you?

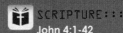

Aa DEFINITION:::

One of the parts of the body by means of which animals stand and walk. [note: the dictionary is clear that "shake a leg" means "to hurry." It does NOT refer to a possible form of entertainment used by airborne soldiers.] Alternate definition: non-airborne.

SCRIPTURE:::
John 4:1-42

"A Samaritan woman came to draw water, and Jesus said to her, "Give me a drink." The Samaritan woman said to him, "How is it that you, a Jew, ask a drink of me, a woman of Samaria?" (Jews do not share things in common with Samaritans.) Jesus answered her, "If you knew the gift of God, and who it is that is saying to you, "Give me a drink.' you would have asked him, and he would have given you living water."

(Also John 8:48-49)

STORY:::

From the first day the black hats instilled the pride of Airborne and the shame of leg land. Remember?

"Whadda ya wanna be!?!", the Black Hat shouted. "AIRBORNE!", thundered back the newest Airborne class. "Whadda ya really, really wanna be!?" he shouted back in response. "Super-Duper Paratrooper, Sergeant. AIRBORNE!", yelled the class. "But what ARE you?", the Black Hat continued. "Dirty, Nasty, Stinking Legs, Sergeant. Airborne!" the class responded with voices stripped of pride. Or running in formation singing, "Dirty Legs, oh how they smell..."

Believe it or not, it was the same in Jesus' day. Back then legs were called Samaritans. The Airborne types, known as Jews, would not speak to Samaritans. They'd step to the other side of the street to avoid social contact. When Jews spoke the word Leg, make that Samaritan, they would utter a curse and spit on the ground. The feeling was mutual.*

Yet it was a Samaritan woman with whom Jesus spoke at the well. It was a Samaritan he held up as the example of good neighbor. And when asked if he himself was a Samaritan, Jesus did not deny it. He truly came for everyone: Jew and Samaritan, Airborne and Leg.

*This background material on Samaritans came from The Disciple Bible Study Manual, published by The United Methodist Church.

AUTHOR'S NOTE:::

Blood wings refers to the practice of pinning on the first set of wings without using the clasps at the back of the needle-like posts that go through the uniform cloth. The wings then are "tapped" to make sure they are securely fastened. The practice is officially discouraged.

FOR REFLECTION:::

Pain of the blood wings aside, remember how good it felt to earn your wings, to become part of a special group? What would help you have that same feeling about being part of God's family?

Which is more difficult for you, the jump from an aircraft while in flight or the leap of faith to believe in the Lord? Why?

Aa DEFINITION:::

A group of people working together in a co-ordinated effort. Teamwork: joint action by a group of people, in which individual interests are subordinated to group unity and efficiency.

SCRIPTURE:::
1 Cor. 12:4-13:13

For just as the body is one and has many members, and all the members of the body, though many, are one body, so it is with Christ... If all were a single member, where would the body be? ...the members of the body which seem to be weaker are indispensable... God has so arranged the body...that there may be no discord in the body, but that the members may have the same care for one another.

(See also Romans 12:3-13)

STORY:::

Once there was a time when everyone wore the same color beret. It showed they were all on the same team. But all was not well.

There were some people with an extra tab or two on their sleeves. They began to argue that they were the most important part of the team. Theirs were the dangerous missions. They took greater risks and had more qualifications than others.

Times changed. There were some people, ones without extra tabs, wearing the beret who did not look like they should be wearing that color beret. So, even though they were part of the team, they were made to wear another color beret.

Some non-tabbed people liked this. At least they were wearing the beret they had earned. Others thought it was awful. It meant they really were not considered part of the team. Their morale plummeted.

The story of two berets raised the question again. Which part of the team is most important: tabbed, staff, or support?

AUTHOR'S NOTE:::

For a time, everybody assigned to a Special Forces unit wore the Green Beret. The Special Forces tab, worn on the left sleeve of the uniform, marked those members of the unit who were Special Forces qualified. Now the Green Beret goes only to those who have earned the tab. Other members of the unit wear the maroon beret of Airborne troops, the tan beret of Rangers, or the black beret of soldiers.

Which part of the Special Forces team can be eliminated: A Teams, B Teams, C Teams, Support Company? What can you do to improve the spirit of teamwork in a community like Special Forces, your unit, or post, or chapel, or family? What does it take to see even the least qualified player as part of the team?

the old man

Aa DEFINITION:::

[slang] One's father; one's husband; anyone in authority, as the head of a company, captain of a vessel, or military commander. Someone who is wise.

SCRIPTURE:::
Isaiah 40:29-31

He gives power to the faint, and strengthens the powerless. Even youths will faint and be weary, and the young will fall exhausted; but those who wait for the Lord shall renew their strength, they shall mount up with wings like eagles, they shall run and not be weary, they shall walk and not faint.

STORY:::

In a Non-Qualified Personnel (NQP) program, a National Guard pre-SFAS (Special Forces Assessment and Selection) effort, the soldiers were anxious to learn about the spirit required to be SF. Gathered in front of a short, 15-foot rope climb, an instructor told them there were several climbing techniques from which to choose.

One method was hand-over-hand, using purely arm strength to reach the top. "Monkey style," using hands and feet together in a way that was almost impossible on slick rope, was next. The final possibility was mockingly called "old man style."

A white-templed, 57-year-old sergeant demonstrated the last style. As he locked his feet into the rope in a way that created a series of "steps" that took him to the top you could see it in the eyes of the soldiers. This was the sissy way. They would go hand-over-hand, or not at all.

Many were good at it, quickly pulling themselves to the top. Others struggled, but got there. All of them were kept at the rope climb until their arm strength was gone. Then the group moved to the next teaching point. There, previously hidden by tall trees and a bend in the trail, was a 50 foot rope climb. There everyone learned the "old man style." It was the best technique for the long haul, and for the short haul with heavy loads.

SF: Special Forces

Some believers are flashy. They use a "hand-over-hand" kind of faith to pull themselves through life, relying solely on their own strength. How well does that describe your spiritual life?

The "old-man style" of believing is marked by faithful attendance at worship; a deliberate prayer life; tithing one's time, talent, and income; serving God daily; making pilgrimages; and an openness to spiritual growth. It gets one to the high places. What parts of this style do you still need to learn? What will help you learn?

Aa DEFINITION:::

The insignia worn by pilots and crew of military aircraft; the insignia airborne and air assault soldiers wear to indicate their qualification.

SCRIPTURE:::
Philippians 3:1

....but this one thing I do: forgetting what lies behind and straining forward to what lies ahead, I press on toward the goal for the prize of the heavenly call of God in Christ Jesus.

STORY:::

Believers speak of badges of faith, prizes they will one day receive: eternal life; the kingdom of heaven; and angel's wings. They are prizes that seem remote, unreachable, or not worth pursuing. But stop to remember.

Go back to Ft. Benning, or the site of your Airborne training, and remember the pursuit of those silver jump wings. It was only a three-week program, but often the wings seemed remote, even unattainable. Every day there were reasons to quit.

Muscles burned midst another set of pushups. Ill-fitting parachute training harnesses bruised shoulders and rubbed skin raw. Fingers and knuckles were swollen from grabbing the risers on the swing landing trainer. Legs felt like lead from climbing the 34-foot towers and doing countless PLFs. Lungs gasped for air midst the chants of the four-mile formation runs.

Every day there seem to be reasons to give up being a person of faith, one of God's chosen people. A financial appeal from a storm-ravaged area taps money set aside for personal use. The Sabbath would be more restful without going to community worship. Scripture study takes time from one's hobby. Tithing takes too much money and not doing it makes one feel guilty. It's too hard being different from everyone else.

Still, the prize is out there. Wings. Remote they may be, but two things, at least, are certain. 1) No one can make us forgo the prize. Only we ourselves can quit. 2) Wings are earned one day at a time. Each day brings both an opportunity to say, "No!" and a chance to say, "Yes!"

God's call is to remain faithful. Always saying, "Yes!" to God earns the wings, the prize. It costs much, but not doing so costs even more. Not doing so costs our souls.

What makes you want to quit being faithful?

How do you fight the temptation to quit? What keeps you going for another day? How do you help others keep faith along with you?

Aa DEFINITION:::

1. A small, rough building or lean-to, used for shelter 2. A large barn-like or hangar-like structure, often with open front or sides 3. To cast off or lose, to get rid of.

SCRIPTURE:::

Matthew 6: 8-15

Our Father in heaven, may your name be hallowed; .... Forgive us the wrong we have done, as we have forgiven those who have wronged us...

For if you forgive others the wrongs they have done, your heavenly father will also forgive you.

STORY:::

The harness shed there at Ft. Benning's Lawson Field is over 50 years old. Thousands of fledgling paratroopers have stood in those aisles and sat on those benches. Can you go there in your mind? Where did you sit? What color were the lines painted? Were you there when it was too hot or too cold?

It is axiomatic that no airborne soldier is ever afraid to jump out of what "legs" refer to as a perfectly good airplane. Psychologists and others who study the mechanisms we use to cope with fear tell us two common coping techniques are talking and sleeping. Since none of us was afraid there in the harness shed, that may be why they had those two rules: 1) No Talking in the Harness Shed! 2) No Sleeping in the Harness Shed! Not being afraid, or even nervous, about those first jumps meant there was no need for us to either talk or sleep, even during weather delays.

Of all the things I remember about the harness shed, the thing that stands out the most is the voice booming out over the PA system, "Quiet in the harness shed! No talking!" Then a moment later, with everyone rigged for a combat equipment jump, "On your feet! No talking in the harness shed! Beat your boots!"

Somehow, though, once I got my wings none of what happened in the harness shed seemed to matter anymore. It wasn't that I forgot; it was, in the words of a friend, "that I remembered it no more against them." Shed of what had been burdensome feelings, I was able to forgive -- to remember it no more against them.

Note: A new harness shed now exists at Lawson Field.

Beat your boots!: Knee bends, reaching down to slap one's boots.

 FOR REFLECTION:::

Where are those places in your life where you have felt misused and unable to respond?

What do you do with the frustration or anger that builds when someone has you toeing a line that you don't think is right?

How hard is it for you to forgive? How does thinking of forgiveness as "remembering it no more against them" change your understanding of it?

What do you need to shed in order to forgive -- and be forgiven?

SECTION SIX:::
ARMY
VALUES

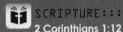

FRANK

Aa DEFINITION:::
Open and honest in expressing what one thinks or feels; straightforward; candid. An Army value.

SCRIPTURE:::
2 Corinthians 1:12
Indeed, this is our boast, the testimony of our conscience: we have behaved in the world with frankness and godly sincerity, not by earthly wisdom but by the grace of God.

STORY:::
I always knew him as Uncle Frank. He was an uncle by friendship rather than blood, being godparent to my younger sister, and there with me at several graduations after Dad died. He was big, tall, and physically strong, but also quiet and gentle. You listened when he spoke, partly because it caught you by surprise, but mostly because when he talked he had something worth saying. He was open and honest, always straightforward. He was, like his name, frank.

On June 6, 1944 the 5th Ranger battalion was pinned down by heavy enemy fire on bloody Omaha beach. As Brigadier General Cota moved along the beach he came to the rangers. "What outfit is this?" he shouted. "We're rangers, Sir!" came back the reply. BG Cota's response, slightly altered, has become the motto of today's Rangers, "Rangers, lead the way!"

Two soldiers shoved a bangalore torpedo forward and blew a hole in the wire. 2LT Francis Dawson was first through the wire. He ran through an uncleared minefield and personally destroyed the pillbox blocking the advance. He led the way off the beach, was awarded the Distinguished Service Cross, later retired as a colonel, and is one of the original members in the Ranger Hall of Fame.

The Rangers knew him as Bull Dawson. But I've always known him as Uncle Frank.

AUTHOR'S NOTE:::
Colonel Frank Dawson died of cancer on October 18, 1997. He is missed.

FOR REFLECTION:::

Name the quiet, honest people who have made a difference in your life. List the good traits about them that somehow you know you were meant to copy.

What uncleared minefields (dangerous, scary places) in your personal life must you cross before you can lead the way for others?

What will it take for you to be always frank – open and honest? Where will you find the wisdom and courage to be that way?

DEFINITION:::

The acronym that stands for Mission Essential Task List. The list, as the name implies, specifies those things that each unit in the army must do to accomplish its mission.

SCRIPTURE:::
Matthew 22:33-40

One of them, a lawyer, asked him a question to test him. "Teacher, which commandment in the law is the greatest?" He [Jesus] said to him, "You shall love the Lord your God with all your heart, and with all your soul, and with all your mind.' This is the greatest and first commandment. And a second is like it. 'You shall love your neighbor as yourself.' On these two commandments hang all the law and the prophets." (Also: Luke 10:25-28 Deuteronomy 6:5 Leviticus 19:18)

STORY:::

It was the middle of an AAR following a long, arduous rotation at JRTC. People were huddled around the one OC who really seemed to be knowledgeable. There was something about him. He spoke with authority, but it was more than that. His answers to questions always focused on what was most important.

Someone threw a loaded question at the OC. "Out of all the things we have to do to be ready, what is most important?" he was asked. It was a barracks lawyer question, one meant to trip up the OC and maybe even get the question asker out of some work.

"The most important thing to do," he said, "is your METL. Every regulation, training manual, field circular, DA pamphlet, everything hangs on the Mission Essential Task List. Do that and you'll be all you can be."

AAR: After-action Report

JRTC: Join Readiness Training Center

OC: Observer Controller

DA: Department of the Army

FOR REFLECTION:::

Jews and Christians have much the same METL. Jesus quoted from the Hebrew Scriptures (Old Testament) when he said that the greatest commandment of all was to love God with all of one's heart, soul, mind and strength. And that a second commandment was equally critical: to love one's neighbor as one's self. That's the METL for believers.

Does your physical exercise program enable you to give all of your strength to God, or are you sitting around with no real strength, stamina, or flexibility? What do you need to change so you are physically fit enough to love God with all the strength within you? What about your spiritual exercise program, so that you give all of your soul? Or your mental development program so that you offer an ever sharper and more discerning mind? Do you have an emotional growth program (like counseling, therapy, etc.) so you bring to God a stronger heart? What evidence shows you love your neighbor, and how do you honestly feel about yourself?

JUMPER

Aa DEFINITION:::
A person who jumps. Jump is defined as: to spring into the air; to start out or forward; to move energetically; to rise suddenly in rank or status.

SCRIPTURE:::
Hebrews 11:1;12:1; 13:6
Now faith is the assurance of things hoped for, the conviction of things not seen...
Therefore, since we are surrounded by so great a cloud of witnesses, let us also lay aside every weight and the sin that clings so closely, and let us run with perseverance the race that is set before us...
So we can say with confidence, "The Lord is my helper; I will not be afraid. What can anyone do to me?"

STORY:::
It was by faith that I made my first jump out of that C-130 flying at 1,250 feet. My conviction was that the unseen parachute would properly deploy. That first jump was difficult; it took courage and trust. But it was a jump that had lots of preparation behind it. Long before, people asked me to think about jump school. When I first commited to become a jumper, others told me, in great detail, what to expect there. At the school there was intensive instruction, the fellowship of struggling together, singing airborne "hymns" as we ran (only some of which could have been used in church), and participation in the regular rituals of airborne drills. I made that first jump because I was prepared for it, I wanted to join those who were already jump-qualified, and I wanted the experience myself.

Since that first jump, I have grown in my appreciation of the airborne community. What seemed a crazy thing to do back then has changed in character. It is now a defining part of my life. Without that leap of faith, my life would be impoverished.

This airborne journey is a model of a faith journey, too. Long before I made my first real leap of faith, there were people of the faith community encouraging me. They told me how it was for them and sang songs that stirred the heart and challenged the soul. There were even periods of intense instruction (Sunday School, VBS, Revivals, etc.). When I made my first leap of faith, it was with the consciousness that I was joining a significant group of people who led the way for me. It was, though, a choice I made personally. As with my airborne jumping, there was no way I could have known, at the time of my first leap of faith, how richly my life would come to be blessed.

VBS: Vacation Bible School

AUTHOR'S NOTE:::
Airborne troops must jump at least once every three months to be "current." Failure to do so means loss of monthly jump pay – a "pay hurt."

Have you made the jump of faith? If not, what help do you need to make that jump? What is your plan for getting that help?

If it has been a long time since your last leap of faith, you need to attend a jump refresher course to regain current jump status. That refresher course might include attending church, finding a fellowship group, and a number of other possibilities. How much of a refresher do you need? If you are currently on "jump status," make sure you aren't a "pay hurt."* You should be drawing some real dividends from your jumps of faith. If you aren't, you might be a pay hurt. How will you get current?

*Soldiers on jump status receive extra pay. If they don't jump often enough (stay current), they lose that pay.

Regulations

Aa DEFINITION:::
Authoritative rules dealing with details or procedure; rules or orders having the force of law issued by an executive authority of a government.

SCRIPTURE:::
Deuteronomy 30:15-20
Today I offer you the choice of life and good, or death and evil. If you obey the commandments of the Lord your God which I give you this day, by loving the Lord your God, conforming to his ways, and keeping his commandments, statutes and laws, then you will live. . . Choose life

STORY:::
Where I read it, I can't recall, but the described difference between the former Soviet Union's army and our army stuck with me. It went like this: In the Soviet army if it is not specifically permitted by regulations, then it is prohibited. In the United States Army if it is not specifically prohibited by regulations then it is permitted.

Another way to describe the differences would be to raise two questions. First, "Where does it say you can?" Second, "Where does it say I can't?" These different approaches to regulations were said to be the strongest reasons for the lack of freedom there and the incredible freedom we enjoy in the United States.

One reason frequently given by God's people for not being more active in their communities of faith (be it synagogue or church), or for not journeying further in the faith, is this: "I don't want to be told what I can do." It's the same reason some people give for not becoming persons of faith in the first place.

One of our best-kept secrets as God's people living in difficult, dangerous days is the freedom we have because of our approach to regulations. The pitfalls that lead to spiritual death are clearly marked. They are prohibited. Everything else is territory we may walk as we live out our faithful love of God, neighbor, and self. We are freed for joyful obedience.

💡 FOR REFLECTION:::

Have you been looking at faith as something that puts you in a straight-jacket or something that sets you free?

What things have you been doing that you know should be prohibited?

What things have you not been doing that you should permit yourself to do?

How are you surprised by the idea that regulations can set us free?

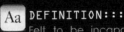

Aa DEFINITION:::
Felt to be incapable of being done, attained, or fulfilled.

SCRIPTURE:::
Mark 10:27
Jesus looked at them and said, "For mortals it is impossible, but not for God; for God all things are possible."

STORY:::
It's almost an article of faith in the army: "The difficult we do immediately, the impossible takes a little bit longer." Consider a simple story of underwear.

The boy, perhaps seven years old, lived in one of the poorest sections of hurricane-ravaged Florida City. Even before Hurricane Andrew, that was one of the poorest cities in the country. National Guard soldiers handed his family emergency food supplies and provided some basic medical care. One soldier, wanting to find out if there were other needs, knelt before the boy, looked into his eyes, and asked what he needed most.

There was no electricity. Food supplies only trickled in. Flash-lights and batteries were popular. Many children wanted toys. The boy could have asked for anything, but he asked for underwear.

School would start soon, signaling a return to normalcy and bringing the hope of a future made better by education. Underwear would make him feel good about going to school.

Pain filled the soldier's eyes as he passed the story on in his unit. Getting underwear seemed impossible. But the story was retold elsewhere and proved to be a catalyst. Some 400 miles away it inspired people in a community of faith. People in the church responded by purchasing over 700 pairs of underwear for children in that boy's school.

What seemed impossible became reality because a soldier cared enough to kneel down and ask a little boy a question. It also happened because the same soldier was brave enough to share his pain and tears with the other soldiers of his unit.

PT: Physical Training

Remember things that seemed impossible when you first looked at them (maxing the PT test, completing your degree, making it through Ranger school, patching up that broken relationship, etc.). Where did you get the courage to try anyway?

Where do you find a network of faithful friends who will help you when times are tough? When are you most likely to ask God for help? (Note: Sometimes when we share a painful story with others, like the soldier did about underwear for the little boy, that's a form of prayer.)

Describe the different kinds of prayer you know about. What keeps you from praying more often?

Aa DEFINITION:::

One that is antagonistic to another; a military adversary; a hostile unit or force.

STORY:::

Joshua Chamberlain led Union troops from the state of Maine at the Battle of Gettysburg. His bravery and ability to command enabled the Union to hold Little Round Top, win at Gettysburg, finally, to win the war. Wounded six times, he received the Medal of Honor, and finished the war as a general. In honor of their heroism, General Grant chose Chamberlain's troops to accept the final Confederate surrender. Chamberlain had helped win the war; now he and his troops were to help secure the peace.

The Civil War was a bitter struggle. Counting the losses on both sides, there were some 954,000 casualties, of which 624,000 were deaths, in its four years. After such horrendous fighting, how could the newly restored nation bind its wounds? The answer came in the words of Confederate general John B. Gordon at the surrender at Appomatox Courthouse:

We were ragged and had no shoes. The banners our Army had borne to the heights of Gettysburg were bloody and in shreds...We were only the shadow of an army, the ghost of an army, and as we marched in tattered hungry columns between those magnificent straight lines of well-fed men, faultlessly armed and perfectly equipped, most of us wished, as our great chief did, that we might have numbered with the fallen in the last battle... Suddenly I heard a sharp order down that blue line, and on that instant I saw the whole brigade present arms to us—to us, the survivors of the Army of Northern Virginia. It was a Maine brigade, comrades, and I confess to you that....I never hear the name of that state but that I feel a certain swelling pride as I reflect that there was an army good enough to deserve that salute—and another magnanimous enough to give it.

AUTHOR'S NOTE:::

See 'Hope Is Not a Method', by former Army Chief of Staff Gordon R. Sullivan and Michael V. Harper, pp. 240-241, for a more complete telling of this story.

FOR REFLECTION:::

When you have been hurt (wounded) by others, what keeps you from ending (killing) the relationship?

When someone asks to be forgiven, do you carry a grudge or salute them for their courage? What keeps you from being stuck-up, self-righteous, and arrogant when you win? How do you love your enemy?

Aa DEFINITION:::
A small vessel propelled by oars, or paddles (or rifle butts!) or by sail or power.

SCRIPTURE:::
Matthew 8:23-27
And when Jesus got into the boat, his disciples followed him. A windstorm arose on the sea, so great that the boat was being swamped by the waves; but Jesus was asleep. And they went and woke him up, saying, "Lord, save us! We are perishing!" And he said to them, "Why are you afraid, you of little faith?" Then he got up and rebuked the winds and the sea; and there was a dead calm. They were amazed, saying, " What sort of man is this, that even the wind and the sea obey him?"

STORY:::
Naval gunfire roared overhead. Incoming rounds sent geysers of water rushing skyward. Automatic weapons fire chattered up ahead. And the boat tossed miserably on the waves, pushed by wind and sea alike. Huddled on the personnel deck of the landing craft some soldiers prayed, "God, if you get me out of this, I'll never doubt again." It was D-Day. Orders told them, "Go!"

At another time a worried U.S. Life Saving Service (the forerunner of today's Coast Guard) crew stared at the raging angry sea. Crashing waves sent foam flying and stirred a bubbling cauldron of water about their feet. Called to launch their oar-driven boat to attempt rescue of a sinking ship's crew, one of their number balked. "If we get in that boat, we'll never come back!', he cried. The skipper shouted over the storm's fury, "Orders don't say a d--- thing about coming back. They say you go!"

Being around boats is risky business. Boats are mentioned some 46 times in the Bible, 43 of those in the Christian scriptures– and in those stories people either heard Jesus or saw a miracle every time they were around boats. And when the disciples got in a boat with Jesus, they always got a miracle. It can be scary, but get in the boat with Jesus– and the orders do say "Go!"– and you'll see a miracle, too.

AUTHOR'S NOTE:::
A special thanks to the soldiers of the 159th Transportation Battalion (Boat). You were aways kind to the battalion commander's son. And in memory of Colonel Paul H. Miller, TC, USA, who taught his son many things.

FOR REFLECTION:::

What would it take for you to get in the boat and face D-Day or a raging storm? Remember a time when you did the right thing without being sure how it would turn out. How did you feel inside?

Jesus calmed the wind and the sea simply by speaking a word. What word must he speak to calm the storm(s) in your life? Hear him say that word. Listen carefully. It comes to you through the howling wind. Hear him.

uniform

Aa DEFINITION:::

Having always the same form, manner or degree; dress of a distinctive design or fashion worn by members of a particular group and serving as a means of identification.

SCRIPTURE:::
1 Samuel 38-43, 48-50

Saul clothed David with his armor; he put a bronze helmet on his head and clothed him with a coat of mail. David strapped Saul's sword over the armor, and he tried in vain to walk, for he was not used to them. Then David said to Saul, "I cannot walk with these; for I am not used to them." So David removed them... So David prevailed over the Philistine with a sling and a stone, striking down the Philistine and killing him.

STORY:::

Uniforms are interesting. They tell you at a glance where someone serves. If you are reasonably knowledgeable, a Class A uniform can even tell you the soldier's length of service, accomplishments, and places served.

Uniforms are interesting another way. While they reveal many things, they also hide even more. The college graduate from a wealthy family stands next to, and is indistinguishable from, the high school dropout from the wrong side of the tracks. Basic training haircuts even give everyone the same hairstyle. For some, the chance to blend in is a chance to start over.

There are even "uniforms" of sorts in places besides the military and law enforcement. For thousands of people who served on the home front during World War II, there was special clothing worn in factories. Rosie the Riveter was as much in uniform as any G.I. For students at church schools, there are often uniforms. Even at public schools students don uniforms as they proclaim to their parents, "But this is what everyone is wearing!"

There is another thing about uniforms. No matter how similar they are, people find ways to let their distinctive personalities shine through. Sometimes it is the tilt of a hat, the shine of the shoes, or the ignoring of ribbons. Often it is the confidence of one's stride, the snappiness of a salute, or the freshness of a smile. Who we are shines through any uniform we may ever wear.

FOR REFLECTION:::

As God's people in today's world, we are called upon to be readily identifiable. What uniform identifies you as one of God's people, or do most people have no idea you are a believer?

How does God's light and love shine through you? Do you train with your spiritual weapons regularly, or do they mostly sit in an armorer's vault chained to a rack and unused? Do you have the right uniform for the environment in which you fight? Do you wear your spiritual uniform with pride, or try to stay unnoticed?

Aa DEFINITION:::
The act or duty of protecting or defending; to protect from danger, especially by watchful attention; a shortened form of National Guard, as in "I'm in the Guard."

SCRIPTURE:::
Matthew 25:1-12
Then the kingdom of heaven will be like this. Ten bridesmaids took their lamps and went to meet the bridegroom. Five of them were foolish, and five of them were wise. When the foolish took their lamps, they took no oil with them; but the wise took flasks of oil with their lamps. As the bridegroom was delayed, all of them became drowsy and slept. But at midnight there was a shout, "Look! Here is the bride-groom! Come out to meet him.

STORY:::
Once there were two National Guard soldiers; one was wise and one was foolish. The foolish one received all the training needed to become a good, competent soldier. Pay and benefits were welcomed and quickly used. Issued field gear was scattered randomly around the house. When there was an inspection, and when it was time for annual training, it was always difficult to find it all.

The foolish soldier made no plans for an emergency call-up; no will, no power of attorney, no arrangements for financial obligations. The soldier's spouse had no idea where important papers were, how to pay the bills, or what to do in a family emergency.

The foolish one also stopped staying in good physical condition. The wrong foods crept in. Daily exercises and running slowed and then stopped. When the annual weigh-in and PT test came, the chance of failure was real.

The wise soldier had the same initial training. Pay and benefits were welcomed, invested. Additional training for personal and professional improvement was sought. Equipment was all in good condition, stored properly, and ready to go. The wise soldier planned for emergency call-up, both state activation and federal active duty. Every possibility was considered, prepared for. There was a will, power of attorney, and plans for financial changes. The soldier's spouse was up to speed on bill paying, emergency contacts, and emergency support.

This wise one knew both to look after equipment and to look after physical conditioning. Good diet, regular physical check-ups, and a solid exercise program kept the soldier in shape. The only question on the PT test was how far above the 300 "maximum" score the soldier would go.

Then one day the soldiers were mobilized.

Whether you are active duty, a reservist, or a National Guard soldier, the issues are the same. How are you like the foolish soldier? In what ways are you like the wise soldier? Overall, would you call yourself wise or foolish?

What must you do to become wiser still? When will you start? What will it take for you to always stay ready?

Aa DEFINITION:::

Load Bearing Equipment, a harness-like set of shoulder straps (or suspenders) used by soldiers to carry a wide variety of equipment. Compare with yoke: a frame fitted to a person's shoulder's to carry a load in two equal portions.

SCRIPTURE:::
Matthew 11:28-30

"Come to me, all you that are weary and are carrying heavy burdens, and I will give you rest. Take my yoke upon you, and learn from me; for I am gentle and humble in heart, and you will find rest for your souls. For my yoke is easy, and my burden is light."

STORY:::

Jesus knew about LBE. Call it LBE or LCE (Load Carrying Equipment), it would make no difference. Jesus knew about it.

Jesus looked right through people. He could see the ones who just put on a show. They wore their LBE, but their canteens were never full. Flashlights had no batteries and ammo pouches held empty magazines. These soldiers put on a good outward show, but they were not truly dependable.

He noticed the other kind of soldiers, too. These carried their load, and more. Besides full canteens, working flashlights, and a full load of ammo, these people carried more. Sometimes they added a light item, like ranger (i.e. pace count) beads. Often it was something heavy, carried in case of need, like an extra canteen, or a first aid kit, or survival equipment.

But beyond the gear that anyone could see, Jesus saw the other loads that people carried. The medic whose biggest burden was not the weight of his field gear, but the memory of that life he thought he should have saved. The unit leaders who wore the green tabs easily but who agonized over the weight of soldiers lost in battle. The seemingly carefree soldier whose love relationship just ended. Every hurt and pain, every fear and worry,

Jesus could see all these things Jesus called LBE by a different name. He referred to it as a yoke. But he knew what it was, just the same.

Green tabs: Worn on uniform epaulets to indicate leaders with command responsibilities.

What extra items do you carry on your LBE and why? If you aren't carrying a full load, what keeps you from carrying your fair share?

Did you know Jesus could give you a spiritual yoke to carry the burdens others can't see? What additional instructions do you need to hook your burdens to that spiritual LBE? Remember the way you feel when you remove your heavily laden LBE after wearing it for a long time. Describe that feeling to someone else, or think it through in your own mind, or even put it in writing. Putting your personal burdens on Jesus' LBE brings that same feeling. Go for it.

Aa DEFINITION:::

Impaired by lack of use, neglect; having lost facility through lack of practice.

SCRIPTURE:::
Luke 15:11-32

But while he was far off, his father saw him and was filled with compassion, and he ran and put his arms around him and kissed him. The father said to his slaves, ..."let us eat and celebrate; for this son of mine was dead and is alive again, he was lost and is found!' And they began to celebrate.

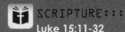 STORY:::

The door to the orderly room banged open. Framed against the blue sky stood a red-haired sergeant. His piercing eyes seeming to measure each occupant. His BDUs told part of the story: Combat Infantryman's Badge; Senior Jump Wings; Aircrew Wings; Drill Sergeant Badge; Recruiter's Badge. Sergeant "Rusty" Smith had come to join the unit.

In after-duty bull sessions, Rusty would fix his eyes on me, a recently commissioned chaplain, and say, "Chaplain, I just want to know one thing. If God was on our side in Vietnam, who was on theirs?" In the twenty years he had been home from that war, his life had not gone well. And in all that time he had never been to church.

His challenges kept coming. Finally I put a challenge before him. If he beat me on the next PT test (my first since joining the Guard) I'd buy him a case of beer. "What happens if you win?" he wanted to know. "Then you have to come to church one time,"

It was an experienced airborne drill sergeant against a green, 1Lt, leg chaplain. We did our pushups and situps side-by-side to keep tabs on one another. When we did the two-mile run I was afraid to slow down.

Chapel was in a large tent, sides rolled up to catch whatever breeze the summer morning offered. Sergeant Smith was there, one foot inside the tent, and the other outside. It was his first chapel service since Vietnam.

At first I thought I'd won the bet, and I did outscore Rusty on the PT test. But since then I've decided that Rusty won. God helped him find a way home to where he really wanted to be. Rusty made sure he would be at chapel. He did the minimum number of pushups and sit-ups required to pass and used almost all of his allotted time on the two-mile run. He lost, but he found.

What parts of your faith life have you neglected? What is rusty from lack of use?

When was the last time you really went home to God? In what ways do you hear God calling you out of the war zones of your life? What do you have to lose in order to find your way home?

light fighter

SECTION SEVEN:::
REUNION

: DATE

: PROMOTE

: SIMPLE

: HOME

: ROE

: INCOMING

: CORDON & SEARCH

: CHANGE

: LIMA BRAVO SIERRA

Welcome home! Your deployment, no matter where it took you, separated you from your family and friends. You served your country at a time of great need.

During your time away, life continued for all those you left at home. You will have stayed in touch with them through letters, e-mail, packages, and phone calls. Now you'll be face-to-face with one another. We wish you the very best reunion possible.

One key to a great reunion is to communicate with each other. So many things happen in a year's time that it's hard to know where to begin the conversation. Experiences will have been so different that sometimes it's hard to find the words to share them, even when you want desperately to do so. Having something that gets the conversation started can be a great help. That's one of the things this section of Light Fighter does.

Aa DEFINITION:::

A particular month, day, and year that something happened or will happen. an appointment, especially a social engagement arranged beforehand; a person with whom one has such an appointment.

SCRIPTURE:::

Mark 13: 32-37
(Jesus is speaking to some of his disciples)

"No one knows about that day or hour, not even the angels in heaven, nor the Son, but only the Father. Be on guard! Be alert! You do not know when that time will come. It's like a man going away: He leaves his house and puts his servants in charge, each with his assigned task, and tells the one at the door to keep watch.

Therefore keep watch because you do not know when the owner of the house will come back – whether in the evening, or at midnight, or when the rooster crows, or at dawn. If he comes suddenly, do not let him find you sleeping. What I say to you, I say to everyone: 'Watch!'"

STORY:::

Some dates just stand out on the calendar. There are, of course, the major holidays. Then there are birthdays and anniversaries. For mobilized soldiers and their families there are some additional dates: the day the phone call came; the date of mobilization; the date of arrival in theater, and most important, the date of return.

Knowing "the date" helps with planning. For example, when the mobilization order gives you four days to report to the mobilization station you focus your planning. You concentrate on the essentials, on the things that have to get done, including the good-byes that need said. You do that whether you're the soldier leaving or the family member remaining at home.

Knowing "the date" does more than just set priorities for the hard work of leaving. When the date of return is posted, it helps with pacing. You learn to do the things necessary to survive, to endure until reunited with loved ones. That can mean sharpening soldier skills for those at the war front. On the home front it may mean developing independence as you do things your partner used to do. On both fronts you know that every passing day brings you one day closer to the reunion you've anticipated since the date of that first call.

Knowing "the date" of return helps people get ready, just like knowing the date of Christmas helps people prepare for that holiday. It builds a sense of excitement and anticipation, just like what children feel as they anticipate opening presents on Christmas Day. "The date" can also bring a let-down, just like many people experience following all the frenzied preparation for Christmas.

FOR REFLECTION:::

Remember the mobilization date and make a list of all the feelings you remember from that time. Include all of them, both the good ones and the bad ones. What things were better than you expected during the deployment? What things were worse?

What hopes and dreams do you have for the date of reunion with loved one(s)? List all the things you're excited about sharing. What are the things that worry you? What things that got you through the deployment do you need to hang on to during the reunion?

Instead of focusing on the date of return, focus on the "date" with whom you are reuniting. List the special things, including times, dates, and places, that will help you renew and strengthen your relationships with your loved one(s). What will you expect of your date? What will your date expect of you?

How are you doing on your "deployment" here on earth? What preparations have you made for what you are called to do in your life? How are you preparing for your eventual return to your heavenly home? What dates do you keep with God, to nurture and strengthen your relationship with God?

Aa DEFINITION:::

To encourage to exist or flourish (to promote a good relationship); to advance in rank, position, etc.; to encourage the sales, acceptance, or recognition of.

SCRIPTURE:::

John 3:16 "**For God so loved the world that he gave his only Son, so that everyone who believes in him may not perish but may have eternal life.**"

Luke 14:7-11 **For all who exalt themselves will be humbled, and those who humble themselves will be exalted.**"

Mark 10:45 "**For the Son of Man came not to be served but to serve, and to give his life a ransom for many.**"

Romans 5:6-8 **For while we were still weak, at the right time Christ died for the ungodly. 7 Indeed, rarely will anyone die for a righteous person—though perhaps for a good person someone might actually dare to die. 8But God proves his love for us in that while we still were sinners Christ died for us.**

STORY:::

Soldiers deploying in support of Operation Enduring Freedom and Operation Iraqi Freedom often earned more than a combat patch. They found themselves promoted, advancing in rank because the position they occupied called for the higher rank, and because some of the peace-time bureaucratic rules were relaxed. The promotions were earned, they just came sooner than expected.

There were other kinds of promotion besides extra stripes or an additional bar. There were the many ways in which people, despite the miles and time zones separating them, promoted the growth of their relationships. Letters, e-mails, and phone calls kept people connected. Packages helped them feel well cared for. Souvenirs sent from overseas let folks back home know they were remembered. All these things promoted relationships. They helped love between individuals flourish.

God deployed Jesus on Operation Eternal Freedom. God loved us so much that God sent Jesus to help us cut through all the rules and meet the basics required for promotion. While on earth, Jesus worked diligently to promote others, winning for everyone the ultimate promotion of being adopted into God's own family. Jesus loved us so much that he even died for us. It got him promoted to sit at God's right hand – and when we promote our relationship with Jesus, it also brings us, at the end of our days, into God's presence. Now there's a promotion!

 **FOR REFLECTION:::**

In what ways have you promoted your relationship with your loved one? Whether you deployed or remained home, what things do you routinely do to help love flourish between you and your loved ones? What special things do you do that are beyond the routine?

How do you promote your relationship with God? Make a list of the things you do to help your relationship with God flourish? What things do you need to add to that list to help your love grow even more? In what ways do you promote God to others? How do others see your love for God and learn about God's love for them?

For whom would you be willing to give your life?

DEFINITION:::
Not difficult, easy.

SCRIPTURE:::
Matthew 7:13-14
(Jesus is speaking)
"Enter through the narrow gate; for the gate is wide and the road is easy that leads to destruction, and there are many who take it. For the gate is narrow and the road is hard that leads to life, and there are few who find it."

STORY:::
For once the dictionary got it wrong. It defined simple with the word easy. When you think about it, though, it's just not that simple.

A soldier wanted to lose weight. That meant doing two things: exercising more and eating differently (not necessarily eating less, but eating the right things, and doing so the right way). Simple, but not easy.

The unit deployed overseas to support and participate in combat operations. It required gathering everyone at home station, moving to the mobilization station, getting on a plane, and going. Simple, but not easy.

Returning soldiers and their families eagerly anticipated the reunion. Meet at the armory, get in the car, travel home, take off the uniform, and become a civilian again. Simple, but not easy.

FOR REFLECTION:::

Describe a time when you did something you thought looked simple, only to discover it wasn't as easy as it looked. What feelings do you have when you find yourself unable to immediately do something that seems simple? Make a list of some simple, but not easy things you've learned (snow skiing—turn left, right, and stop; surfing—stand up, balance; stop smoking—just quit, etc.). Describe the things that kept you going as you learned to do those "simple" things.

Now that you've got the "simple but not easy" concept, apply it to these statements: 1) being a Christian is simple, but not easy; 2) being married is simple but not easy and 3) being a parent is simple but not easy.

Aa DEFINITION:::

A house or other place of residence; the place in which one's domestic affections are centered; a person's native place or country.

 SCRIPTURE:::

Revelation 21: 3-4
And I heard a loud voice from the throne saying, "See, the home of God is among mortals. He will dwell with them; they will be his peoples, and God himself will be with them; he will wipe every tear from their eyes. Death will be no more; mourning and crying and pain will be no more, for the first things have passed away."

John 14:23
Jesus answered him, "Those who love me will keep my word, and my Father will love them, and we will come to them and make our home with them.

STORY:::

During deployment overseas soldiers often think of home. Sometimes it's just wanting to be back in the United States, where (depending on the part of the country) things are green, there are no sandstorms, and flak vests, helmets, and weapons aren't needed for travel. Home is a country whose blessings are appreciated all the more because being overseas showed what it was like to live without those blessings.

Sometimes the thoughts of home are more focused. Soldiers think of the house where they live, their room and bed with a real mattress, the nearby bathroom with real toilets, and being able to get whatever they want from the refrigerator. They might also think of hometown restaurants, where they can get food they want without waiting in line forever. Similarly, thoughts of home might bring to mind being able to buy the brand of shaving cream, or toothpaste, or deodorant that they really prefer – again without waiting in line forever.

Thinking of home also brings to mind a soldier's loved ones. Letters, packages, e-mails, and phone calls help, but they aren't the same as being home. Nothing replaces being able to see, hold, and touch the love one. Home, in this sense, is where the heart is.

The Bible mentions the word home more than 150 times. People in far countries yearn to return home. God promises to lead the people home, and even to build a home in the midst of the people.

Where is "home" for you? Is it the place where you now live, or does another place come to mind when you hear the word "home?"

Does God have a home in the midst of where you live and work? What things do you need to do to enable God to build such a place in your life?

What do you and your loved one(s) do to turn your house or apartment into a home? Make a list of all your blessings. Be sure to include on your list all the things you and your loved one(s) learned to appreciate about each other during the time of separation.

Describe how it feels to come home. Describe how it feels to have your soldier back at home.

DEFINITION:::

The mass of eggs in a female fish's ovary; acronym used by the military standing for Rules of Engagement.

STORY:::

The Judge Advocate General Corps, the JAGs of TV fame, teach soldiers about the Rules of Engagement regarding any particular operation. Some of the rules change, being dependent on the situations faced by the soldiers. Some of them, however, are standing rules of engagement. They never change, no matter what. One of the quickest ways of getting into trouble is to violate the Rules of Engagement.

The intent of the Standing Rules of Engagement is to implement the right of self-defense, to provide guidance regarding the use of force, and to be used in peacetime operations other than war, and even in war itself. The rules help people live together in difficult situations and keep things from getting worse. That's really what God tried to do by giving us the Ten Commandments. They're our standing ROE for getting along with God and one another. We violate them at our peril, and doing so quickly gets us into trouble.

Even with the rules, things aren't always easy. When JAGs teach the classes on the ROE they routinely include different scenarios and ask people in the class what actions the ROE permit them to take in particular situations. It's a way of learning the ROE and figuring out what to do before one is confronted by trouble. Learning and knowing how to live God's commandments helps us in the same way.

SCRIPTURE:::

Exodus 20: 1-17
Then God spoke all these words: I am the LORD your God, who brought you out of the land of Egypt, out of the house of slavery; you shall have no other gods before me. You shall not make for yourself an idol, whether in the form of anything that is in heaven above, or that is on the earth beneath, or that is in the water under the earth. You shall not bow down to them or worship them; for I the LORD your God am a jealous God, punishing children for the iniquity of parents, to the third and the fourth generation of those who reject me, but showing steadfast love to the thousandth generation of those who love me and keep my commandments.

FOR REFLECTION:::

How well do you know the Rules of Engagement? Can you name and explain the 10 Commandments? Recall times in your life when you know you have not followed one of the Commandments. What happened to you, even if you didn't "get caught?" Answer the question in terms of your relationship with God, with the other persons involved, and with yourself. Describe what happens when everyone follows the Commandments. What happens when no one does? Describe how thinking of the Ten Commandments as Rules of Engagement helps you think of the commandments differently. How are you going to live them? Remember, they, like the standing ROE, are not optional!

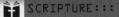

Incoming

Aa DEFINITION:::

Military slang; any rounds of enemy fire, direct or indirect, about to impact on one's location; verbal abuse about to hit oneself or the people in one's area. Flights arriving at an airport.

SCRIPTURE:::

1 Thessalonians 5:1-11
Now concerning the times and the seasons, brothers and sisters, you do not need to have anything written to you. For you yourselves know very well that the day of the Lord will come like a thief in the night. When they say, "There is peace and security," then sudden destruction will come upon them, as labor pains come upon a pregnant woman, and there will be no escape! But you, beloved, are not in darkness, for that day to surprise you like a thief; for you are all children of light and children of the day; we are not of the night or of darkness. So then let us not fall asleep as others do, but let us keep awake and be sober; for those who sleep sleep at night, and those who are drunk get drunk at night. But since we belong to the day, let us be sober...

STORY:::

During their time in the combat theater soldiers learned to tune their ears to certain sounds, particularly those sounds that warned of incoming fire and sudden destruction. It meant the difference between being wounded or not. It even prevented people from being killed, particularly if the warning enabled them to find cover in time.

Family members eagerly awaited the incoming flight. It carried returning soldiers. Tearful, but joyous, reunions stood but moments away. Expectations ran high. Reunited families would resume the lives interrupted by the war-time deployment. They expected things to be good, safe, and secure.

After the initial celebrations, when soldiers and families worked to put their lives back together, sounds of a different kind of incoming were hard to hear. Untrained ears did not pickup the warning of verbal shots about to be fired. Sometimes the returning soldiers got "hit" by family members. Other times the soldier fired "shots" at the family. Depending on their previous experience, those on the receiving end either retreated to safe places, or held their ground and returned fire.

What things set you off and cause you to fire verbal shots without thinking? When are you most likely to negligently discharge your mouth and wound someone with your comments? What can you create to provide a safe way to clear your anger before entering the secure area of your home (remember the clearing barrels)?

What warning sounds do you make before you pop-off a verbal round? How restrictive are your rules of engagement? What do you expect others to do when you fire your anger at them? What do you do when you are on the receiving end? How do you break destructive patterns? How do you stay alert and prepared so you are not caught by surprise? What things can you do to improve your hearing and recognition of the sounds of danger?

DEFINITION:::

(noun) A line of police, warships, etc . guarding and area; (verb) to surround with a cordon. Search – to look through carefully in order to find something.

SCRIPTURE:::

: Luke 15: 4-10

"Which one of you, having a hundred sheep and losing one of them, does not leave the ninety-nine in the wilderness and go after the one that is lost until he finds it? When he has found it, he lays it on his shoulders and rejoices. And when he comes home, he calls together his friends and neighbors, saying to them, 'Rejoice with me, for I have found my sheep that was lost.' Just so, I tell you, there will be more joy in heaven over one sinner who repents than over ninety-nine righteous persons who need no repentance.

STORY:::

: It happened often in Iraq. Soldiers from an infantry unit would cordon off an area then search it carefully, looking for weapons, terrorists, or officials from Saddam Hussein's fallen regime. They were after high value targets.

Every cordon and search involved several elements. The cordon element goes in early, to prevent anyone from escaping. The search element then goes door-to-door, marking off places they've searched so they don't duplicate their efforts. A security element also stands ready, like a quick reaction force, to go where ever it might be needed.

Even in the search element, each team is careful. Someone on the team searches, others pull security. No one works alone.

It turns out that God knows about cordon and search. God constantly searches for, and rejoices in finding, that which is lost.

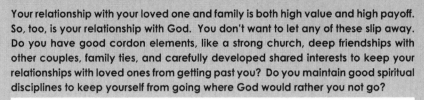

FOR REFLECTION:::

Your relationship with your loved one and family is both high value and high payoff. So, too, is your relationship with God. You don't want to let any of these slip away. Do you have good cordon elements, like a strong church, deep friendships with other couples, family ties, and carefully developed shared interests to keep your relationships with loved ones from getting past you? Do you maintain good spiritual disciplines to keep yourself from going where God would rather you not go?

If things are missing in your relationship, either with loved ones or with God, where do you need to look for them? Who are the people who will help you search? Do you have trained, trusted people to pull security for you as you search? A marriage counselor, family systems therapist, or chaplain can help you here. You may even want a combination of the three.

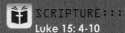

change

Aa DEFINITION:::
(verb) To make or become different; noun – the act, process, or result of changing.

STORY:::
: : It's been said that the only one who likes change is a baby with a dirty diaper, and even then the baby often is crying and screaming throughout the process. Plus, it's messy and smelly for the one making the change.

Here are two more sayings about change. "Change is good, you go first!" "Change is good, unless it happens."

Change happens. It happens to soldiers while they're deployed. It happens to the family members, friends, employers, and all the people who stayed behind while soldiers were gone.

- Babies that were on the way when deployment came will have been born.

- Children can grow three inches in a year and move from being little boys and girls to being young men and women.

- Spouses learn independence and take on tasks the deployed soldier used to do.

- Friends may move away, or

- Soldiers return to jobs that may seem less important and meaningful than before the deployment.

The crazy thing about many of these changes is that everything can look the same, but at the same time be completely different. Crazy, too, is that even good change causes stress.

Here's something else to consider. It comes from a book about change. In the medical world, a clinical definition of death is a body that does not change. Change is life. Stagnation is death. If you don't change, you die. It's that simple. It's that scary.

SCRIPTURE:::
Luke 15: 4-10
"Which one of you, having a hundred sheep and losing one of them, does not leave the ninety-nine in the wilderness and go after the one that is lost until he finds it? When he has found it, he lays it on his shoulders and rejoices. And when he comes home, he calls together his friends and neighbors, saying to them, 'Rejoice with me, for I have found my sheep that was lost.' Just so, I tell you, there will be more joy in heaven over one sinner who repents than over ninety-nine righteous persons who need no repentance.

FOR REFLECTION:::

Describe changes in your life that have been good. What made those changes easier to take?

Now remember and describe some times when bad changes came your way. What healthy things did you do to get through those times? What were some things you tried that didn't help, and that you don't want to do ever again?

Who do you call on to help you in the midst of the change? What other resources do you draw upon? What unchanging things do you count on for stability? What do you do when things get scary?

DEFINITION:::

Lima Bravo Sierra is the military phonetic alphabet for the letters L, B, and S. Those letters form an acronym for which one meaning is, "Lost Biggern' Sin." (Author's note: the actual S-word used in the LBS acronym has four letters and is not appropriate for use in this devotional guide.)

SCRIPTURE:::

Proverbs 4:24-27

Put away from you crooked speech, and put devious talk far from you. Let your eyes look directly forward, and your gaze be straight before you. Keep straight the path of your feet, and all your ways will be sure. Do not swerve to the right or to the left; turn your foot away from evil.

STORY:::

: : The night land navigation exercise gave Pathfinder students the opportunity to lead their group to various coordinates in the woods of Ft. Benning. An instructor accompanied each group, observing students' efforts both in leadership and in map and compass work.

One particular night the student leader got lost, so lost, in fact, that even the accompanying instructor no longer knew their location. When the time by which they were to be at their objective was long past, the instructor made radio contact with the training cadre. The students overheard part of his radio transmission, "Roger, we're LBS. Over."

FOR REFLECTION:::

When have you found yourself lost in life? Think about times when you've been lost travelling. What about times when you weren't sure which direction to take with your life? Who helped you find your way? What did you do to choose the correct path? In the midst of your confusion, what would you have given for a guiding light?

List some times when you and your family have been unsure about what to do. What resources (friends, trained counselors, church, community agencies, etc.) are the ones you most readily use? Which ones might be good to add, just like a GPS unit makes a great addition to the trusty old compass?

light fighter

APPENDIX

- : EMERGENCY RELIGIOUS SUPPORT
- : PRAYERS FOR THE WOUNDED
- : PRAYERS FOR THE DEAD

INTRODUCTION:::

This section provides information about sacraments, rites, and prayers for the wounded and dying. The information source is the Unit Ministry Team (UMT) Handbook, 1990. What follows is copied virtually verbatim from that source.

These sacraments may be administered by either ordained or lay persons when an ordained chaplain of the soldier's own faith is not available. The emphasis in compiling these acts of religious support is on the word 'emergency'. These religious support actions are intended to be short in duration, since time is precious in combat.

If a dying soldier desires religious support, and a chaplain is unavailable, the chaplain assistant, commanding officer, platoon leader, or another soldier may voluntarily repeat with the soldier the prayers given in this section.

EMERGENCY CHRISTIAN BAPTISM:::

If a dying soldier has not been baptized and desires to be and a chaplain is not within reach, any baptized person may administer baptism.
   * Pour water three times on the brow while saying the soldier's first name and this: "I baptize you in the name of the Father, and of the Son, and of the Holy Spirit. Amen."
   * Report the facts to a chaplain as soon as possible.

RELIGIOUS SUPPORT TO THE WOUNDED:::

TO A DYING PROTESTANT SOLDIER
Repeat with the soldier the "Lord's Prayer", the "Apostles' Creed", and the "Prayer for the Sick and Wounded".

The Lord's Prayer. "Our Father who art in heaven, hallowed be Thy name. Thy kingdom come, Thy will be done on earth as it is in heaven. Give us this day our daily bread. And forgive us our trespasses as we forgive those who trespass against us. And lead us not into temptation, but deliver us from evil: For Thine is the Kingdom, and the power, and the glory forever. Amen."

The Apostles' Creed. "I believe in God, the Father almighty, maker of heaven and earth: and in Jesus Christ, his only Son our Lord, who was conceived of the Holy Spirit, born of the Virgin Mary, suffered under Pontius Pilate, was crucified, died, and was buried. He descended into hell; the third day He rose again from the dead. He ascended into heaven and sitteth on the right hand of God, the Father almighty. From thence he shall come to judge the living and the dead. I believe in the Holy Spirit, the holy catholic church, the communion of saints, the forgiveness of sins, the resurrection of the body, and the life everlasting. Amen."

Prayer for the Sick and Wounded. "O Lord, in your mercy behold, visit, and relieve your servant. Give him (her) comfort in the knowledge of your love and sure confidence in your care. Defend him (her) from the danger of the enemy and keep him (her) in spiritual peace and safety; through our Lord Jesus Christ. Amen."

TO A DYING CATHOLIC SOLDIER
Repeat "The Hail Mary", "The Act of Contrition", and "The Sign of the Cross" with the soldier.

The Hail Mary. "Hail Mary, full of Grace! The Lord is with Thee: blessed art thou among women, and blessed is the fruit of thy womb Jesus. Holy Mary, Mother of God, pray for us sinners, now and at the hour of our death. Amen."

The Act of Contrition. "O my God, I am heartily sorry for having offended Thee, and I detest all my sins, because of Thy just punishments, but most of all because they have offended Thee, my God, Who art all good and deserving of all my love. I firmly resolve, with the help of Thy Grace, to sin no more, and to avoid the near occasions of sin. Amen."

The Sign of the Cross. "In the name of the Father, and of the Son, and of the Holy spirit. Amen."

TO A DYING JEWISH SOLDIER
Repeat with the soldier "The Shema", "The Confession for the Critically Ill", and "The 23rd Psalm".

The Shema. "Hear O Israel: the Lord our God, the Lord is One."

The Confession for the Critically Ill. "Lord my God, God of my fathers, before Thee I confess that in Thy hand alone rests my healing or my death. If it be thy will, grant me a perfect healing. Yet if my death be fully determined by Thee, I will in love accept it at Thy hand. Then may my death be an atonement for all sins, transgressions, and for all the wrong which I have committed before Thee. Amen."

The 23rd Psalm. "the Lord is my Shepherd: I shall not want. He maketh me to lie down in green pastures; he leadeth me beside the still waters. He restoreth my soul: he leadeth me in the paths of righteousness for His names's sake. Yea, though I walk through the valley of the shadow of death, I will fear no evil: for Thou art with me: thy rod and thy staff they comfort me. Thou preparest a table before me in the presence of mine enemies; thou annointest my head with oil; my cup runneth over. Surely goodness and mercy shall follow me all the days of my life, and I shall dwell in the house of the Lord forever."

TO A DYING EASTERN ORTHODOX SOLDIER
Repeat with the soldier the following prayers:

- "Holy God! Holy Mighty! Holy Immortal! Have mercy on us." [Repeat this phrase three times.]
- "Glory to the Father, and to the Son, and to the Holy Spirit, now and ever and unto ages of ages. Amen."
- "O Most Holy Trinity, have mercy on us. O Lord, cleanse us from our sins. O Master, pardon our transgressions. O Holy One, visit and heal our infirmities for thy names's sake."
- "Lord, have mercy." [Repeat this phrase three times.]
- "Our Father who art in heaven, hallowed be Thy name. They kingdom come. Thy will be done on earth as it is in heaven. Give us this day our daily bread. And forgive us our trespasses as we forgive those who trespass against us. And lead us not into temptation, but deliver us from the evil one.
- "The Father is my hope, the Son is my refuge, the Holy spirit is my protector. O Holy Trinity, glory to thee."
- "Beneath your compassion we take refuge, O virgin Theotokos. Despite not our prayer in our adversity, but deliver us from harm, O only pure and blessed one."

The following prayer may be substituted for the dying.
- "With the saints give rest, O Christ, to the soul of thy servant, where there is neither sickness nor sorrow, and no more sighing, but life everlasting."

TO A DYING MUSLIM SOLDIER
Repeat with the soldier the "Shahada" and the "Prayers for the Dying".

The Shada. "There is no God but Allah and Mohammed is the messenger of Allah."

Prayers for the Dying.
"Allah is great!" [Repeat this phrase four times.]

- "Oh God, I ask of Thee a perfect faith, a sincere assurance, a reverent heart, a remembering tongue, a good conduct of commendation, and a true repentance, repentance before death, rest at death, and forgiveness and mercy after death, clemency at the reckoning, victory i paradise and escape from the fire, by thy mercy, O mighty One, O Forgiver. Lord increase me in knowledge and join me unto good."
- "O Lord, may the end of my life be the best of it: may my closing acts be my best acts, and may the best of my days be the day when I shall meet Thee."

After a Muslim soldier has breathed his last, his eyes should be gently shut. While closing the eyes of the deceased, one should make the following supplication:
- "O Allah! Make his affair light for him, and render easy what he is going to face after this, and bless him with Thy vision, and make his new abode better for him than the one he has left behind," and in the name of the Spirit who made thee whole. Amen."

PRAYERS FOR THE DEAD:::

In the event of a soldier's death the prayer appropriate to his/her faith may be said.

PRAYER AT THE DEATH OF A PROTESTANT SOLDIER
"Depart, dear brother (sister), out of this world in the name of the Father who created thee, in the name of the Son who redeemed thee, and in the name of the Spirit who made thee whole. Amen."

PRAYER AT THE DEATH OF A CATHOLIC SOLDIER
"Eternal Rest grant unto him (her), O Lord, and let perpetual light shine upon him (her). May his (her) soul and all the souls of the faithful, departed through the Mercy of God, rest in peace."

PRAYER AT THE DEATH OF A JEWISH SOLDIER
"Thy sun shall no more go down neither shall thy moon withdraw itself; for the Lord shall be thine everlasting light, and the days of thy mourning shall be ended. Amen."

PRAYER AT THE DEATH OF AN EASTERN ORTHODOX SOLDIER
"O God of spirits, and of all flesh, who hast trampled down death and overthrown the Devil and given life to thy world; do thou, the same Lord, give rest to the soul(s) of thy departed servant(s) [state soldier's name], in

a place of brightness, a place of refreshment, a place of repose, where all sickness, sighing, and sorrow have fled away. Pardon every transgression which he (she) (they) has (have) committed, whether by word or deed or thought. For thou art a good God and lovest mankind; because there is no man who lives yet does not sin; for thou only art without sin thy righteousness is to all eternity; and thy word is truth. For thou art the Resurrection, the Life, and the Repose of thy servant(s) [state soldier's name] who is (are) fallen asleep, O Christ our God, and unto thee we ascribe glory, together with they Father who is from everlasting, and thine all-holy, good and life-creating Spirit, now and ever and unto ages of ages. Amen."

PRAYERS AT THE DEATH OF A MUSLIM SOLDIER

The person who leads in prayer should stand and face toward Mecca, if possible. The following prayers may be said.

- "Allah is Great!" [Repeat this phrase four times.] "There is no God but Allah and Mohammed is his prophet."
- "Glory be to Thee, O Allah, and I praise Thee. Thy praise is glorified, and there is no God other than Thee."
- "O Allah! Have mercy on Mohammed and on those related to Mohammed, just as Thou hadst mercy and Thou sendst peace and blessed and hadst compassion on Abraham. Surely Thou art Praiseworthy, the Great!"
- "O Allah! Forgive those of us who are still living and those who are dead; those of us who are present and those who are absent, and our minors and our elders. O Allah! Let the one whom thou keepest alive from among us live his life according to Islam, and let the one whom Thou causest to die from among us die as a believer."
- "Peace and Allah's mercy be upon you."

AFTERWORD

afterword

HOW THIS DEVOTIONAL GUIDE GOT STARTED:::

My first battalion commander in Special Forces wanted a good story as part of my report during the daily commander's update briefings at annual training. He kept me thinking and forced me to reach for stories that would connect. Soon I found a rhythm and made a discovery. With stories I could do more than entertain, I could teach.

A single, memorable word with a very short story accompanying it were ways to pinpoint potential trouble areas, clarify values, and occasionally make people laugh. In short, it was a way to take people to church without them knowing they were there and, because of the nature of briefings, without mentioning the scriptures directly and seldom referring to God or Jesus.

While stories built on Words for the Day were finding their way into my tool bag, soldiers were approaching me about their team deployments. "We know you can't be there, Chaplain, but do you have anything we can take with us? There are a lot of believers on our team." So I began to think about a resource aimed at people of faith who wanted to continue their spiritual exercises even in remote places. I typed up some devotions, much like those found here, gave copies to the A Teams headed to places I could not go, and kept the original to use with everyone else.

Those early devotional guides included the ideas that Jesus was infantry, airborne, ranger, and Special Forces qualified. One morning, in a steamy hut in Honduras, I began to tell some soldiers that Jesus was infantry, good old 11B (that's the military occupational specialty [or MOS] for an infantryman). People's ears perked up, even ears that normally did not listen. They were overhearing the gospel without being beaten over the head by it. That may be why Jesus taught in parables. It worked.

The next magic moment came a few days later there in Honduras during 1994 annual training. Our burly, triple-tabbed S-4 piped up and said, "Chaplain, I think Jesus was a pretty good S-4, too. After all, he fed a multitude with few supplies on hand, no organic transportation, and made it look easy." That opened the floodgates: Jesus as an S-1, a medic, and so on.

My hope is that those who already believe will find in this guide a resource that nurtures their faith. Even more, I trust that there will be moments when, through their use of it, some non-believer, or someone whose faith is wavering, will overhear the love their creator has for them and be transformed. By placing the scripture stories into the military environment I hope those in that environment will more and more find themselves in the scriptures and God's love in them.

If you have ideas (for revision or another sequel) or comments to share, please send them to the author via e-mail at jim.foglemiller@us.army.mil.

Chaplain Fogle-Miller

SEQUELS AND SUCH:::

My first devotional guide was entitled SOD-G Special Operations Devotional Guide. The title was a play on SOD-A, otherwise known as Special Operations Detachment -A, or A-Team. The soldiers of 3rd Battalion, 20th Special Forces Group (Airborne), were the target audience. I wrote for them and explained few acronyms or code words because that audience would recognize them all.

Several things happened, though. First, soldiers outside the special operations community got hold of the devotional guide and read it with enthusiasm. Second, reports came in of soldiers sharing the guide with their families, even using them for daily devotion time together. The soldiers described how it helped their families understand what the army was like. That meant two things: a bigger print run during the next printing (the first edition was a limited run of just 500); and a text where all the acronyms were explained.

Before that second printing came a transfer from the Special Forces battalion that had been my home for four years to the 53rd Infantry Brigade. Experience with the conventional side of the house brought more devotions to mind. Strong encouragement came from several sources to do a reprint of the devotional guide. But a simple reprint, even with earlier mistakes corrected and all the unusual terms explained, did not seem right.

The U.S. Army depends upon all of its components, just like the army of God depends on the good people of a variety of denominations and faiths. Without the effort of all of us, the mission does not get accomplished. Thus was born the idea for Light Fighter, an expanded devotional guide that added a new collection of devotions to all the original devotions found in SOD-G.

Thanks go to the men and women of the 53rd Infantry Brigade, Florida Army National Guard, and all who fight for the light anywhere.

ABOUT THE AUTHOR:::

Chaplain Fogle-Miller is an army brat who, like many with similar experiences, has no one place to call home. Becoming an Army National Guard Chaplain in 1986 put him in a familiar uniform among people who felt like home. He felt richly blessed by the experience. Chaplain Fogle-Miller retired effective 31 May 2012 after a final mobilization tour as the I Corps (Rear) (Provisional) Chaplain at Joint Base Lewis-McChord. **Continued on next page>>**

In March of 1992, Chaplain Fogle-Miller was attached to 3rd Battalion, 20th Special Forces Group (Airborne). Though still a "Leg," he survived annual training in July (including heli-casting). That was quickly followed by a month-long deployment
to south Florida for humanitarian support operations following Hurricane Andrew. Three weeks after returning home he was sent, at age 42, to the Airborne Course, which he successfully completed. It was, he noted, good for his prayer life.

After four years with the Special Operations community, the chaplain moved to the conventional side of the house, where he served for over 6 years as the deputy brigade chaplain in the 53rd Infantry Brigade (Separate). He served with the 32d AAMDC in Kuwait and Iraq during OIF1 and deployed to Afghanistan in 2005 as the senior chaplain with the 53rd Infantry Brigade's Task Force Phoenix, after which he became the JFHQ State Chaplain for the Florida National Guard. He still sees large open fields drop zones. Clear, blue-skied days with little wind bring the thought, "This would be a good day for a jump."

In the civilian world, the author and his wife, Beth, are both United Methodis clergypersons. She continues to serve as a pastor in the Florida Conference of the United Methodist Church. Chaplain Fogle-Miller retired not only from the military, but also as a pastor. He stays busy working on the next chapter of his life. Married for over 30 years, he and Beth have one child, a daughter named Carlene, who soon graduates from college. At the tender age of 18 months, she learned how to play "Airborne" and "Airborne-in-the-sky." For the uninitiated, in "Airborne" Carlene would leap from a counter, car top or other high place into her father's arms (feet and knees together, of course). "Airborne-in-the Sky" meant Dad held her under her arms, tossed her into the air, and caught her as she came down. His heart was warmed by the trust she showed and his mind was amazed at her courage. Now far too big and grownup for those games, she still displays courage, trust, and other qualities that would make any parent proud.

For those interested in such things, the author is a 1972 graduate of the University of North Carolina--Chapel Hill. In 1978 he received both Master of Divinity and Master of Arts degrees from Duke University. He also earned a Ph.D. in Sociology of Religion from Emory University.

Chaplain Fogle-Miller has received enough military awards that his Army Service Uniform looks respectable. He is pleased to enjoy the privilege of being able to wear either Honduran or Canadian jump wings.

Current as of January, 2013.

AAMDC: Army Air and Missile Defense Command

Made in the USA
Columbia, SC
15 May 2021